TO PAULA,

MAY THESE BOOKS
BE A BLESSING TO
YOU AND YOUR FAMILY

Michael

GOD BLESS!

A Divine Connection
With A Message From God

Volume II

"Michael!" Yes Lord.
"You Have Been Redeemed!"

A Divine Connection With A Message From God

Volume II

"Michael!" Yes Lord. "You Have Been Redeemed!"

By

MICHAEL ANTHONY GAGLIARDI
Lead By The Holy Spirit

© 2010 by Michael Anthony Gagliardi
Web site: http://www.tellmypeoplethetruth.com

Published for the Internet by ebookit.com
http://www.ebookit.com

ISBN-13: 978-1-4566-0102-7

in any form or by any means like electronic, mechanical, photocopy, recording, or any other, except for the all the Bible scriptures and inspirational and motivational Quotes that are contained in this book, without the written permission from the author/publisher.

Unless otherwise noted, all Bible scriptures are from the New International Version of the Bible.

To the loving memories of my wonderful father, Capt. Leon S. Gagliardi "Capt Leon", my wonderful grandparents, Rev. Oliva Bedard and Monique Bedard, my wonderful aunt Marie Conn and my wonderful father in-law Clarence "Wendell" Powell. You all are so truly missed by everyone and we know you all are rejoicing in Heaven.

Dedication

I am dedicating this book series volume II also to my mother, Paulette L. Gagliardi. She has always been such a great ambassador of the Lord. Since we were born she has raised us all up in church and always loved us unconditionally. And she did that knowing, we would learn to know and understand the real and only truth, which are the living words of God. That is the best gift that anyone could ever give someone. I love you and thank you for that mom. Praise the Lord our God!

Proverbs 22:6 (KJV) *Train up a child in the way he should go: and when he is old, he will not depart from it.*

Ephesians 6:4 (NLT) *Fathers, do not provoke your children to anger by the way you treat them. Rather, bring them up with the discipline and instruction that comes from the Lord.*

Isaiah 59:21 "*As for me, this is my covenant with them," says the LORD. "My Spirit, who is on you, and my words that I have put in your mouth will not depart from your mouth, or from the mouths of your children, or from the mouths of their descendants from this time on and forever," says the LORD.*

Colossians 3:20 *Children, obey your parents in everything, for this pleases the Lord.*

Acknowledgements

I would like to personally thank the following people (in no particular order), for being such a great inspiration to me and also for being great ambassadors of the Lord Jesus Christ and His Kingdom in Heaven;

Evangelist Billy Graham, Dr. Creflo Dollar, Pastor John Hagee and his Son, Joel Osteen and his Father, Pastor Benny Hinn, Paul Crouch and the PTL family, Joyce Meyer Ministries, Pastor Rod Parsley, Dr. Charles Stanley, Dr. Robert H. Schuller, Jesse Duplantis, Pastor Gregory Dickow, Pat Robertson and the 700 club family, James Robison and his wife Betty, Jack Van Impe Ministries, Evangelist Jimmy Swaggart, Oral Roberts Ministries, my Pastor Jeff Daws at Stockbridge Community Church, my very good friend Dr. Daniel A. Nickles DMD, my friend and mentor Darren Little, my wonderful wife, kids and my grand kids, my wonderful brother and sisters, my wonderful aunts and uncles, my wonderful cousins, my wonderful in-laws and all my personal friends I have met through the years,

A percentage of the net profits of this book will be given to the above ministries, who help the needy and further the kingdom of Heaven.

Malachi 3:10 *Bring the whole tithe into the storehouse, that there may be food in my house. Test me in this," says the LORD Almighty, "and see if I will not throw open the floodgates of heaven and pour out so much blessing that you will not have room enough for it.*

The Power of Giving

Giving is powerful. Many people will attempt to prevent you from taking, yet no one can stop you from giving as much as you wish.

Give and you increase the value that flows through your Life. Give of yourself, and you make yourself stronger.

Every time you interact with someone else, you have the opportunity to give that person some kind of value. Whether it is a thing, or a thought, a gesture or a kind word, the most powerful gifts are those that come straight from the heart.

Many will appreciate your gifts and some will not, but that is not the point. For it is the sincere act of giving, not how the gift is received, that brings value and goodness to your world.

As you give more and more, you have more to give. As the joy of giving flows out from you, new richness fills your life.

Each moment is an opportunity to engage the beautiful loving power of giving. Give your best and you'll get even better.

~Ralph Marston~

14

My prayer to God the Father

I pray to my Heavenly Father, that as all the readers read this book, you will open their minds, hearts and souls, so that they may receive what the Holy Spirit has and will be given me to share with your people. As I write this book, I also asked the Holy Spirit to guide me to write what is truly given to me by God the Father, so that it will help guide them to live a life full of true peace, true love, true joy and true happiness here on earth, until they enter the Kingdom of Heaven.. I also like to thank my Heavenly Father in advance, that you have the opportunity to read this book, in hope that after reading it, you will receive the wisdom and understanding of God and His living words. I ask this in Jesus mighty name, Amen

John16:13 *But when he, the Spirit of truth, comes, he will guide you into all the truth. He will not speak on his own; he will speak only what he hears, and he will tell you what is yet to come.*

About The Author

My name is Michael Anthony Gagliardi. I have a beautiful wife, Missy and three beautiful children, Heather, Chelsea and Cody. I also have a granddaughter; Shatavia and grandson Devontay. I really love, trust and believe in the Lord and His living words with all my heart, mind and soul.

What really inspired me to continue to write more volumes in the same book series was that, I truly feel that I am lead by the Holy Spirit to continue spreading the living words of God to His people before His coming.

I also feel a very strong calling on my life to help God's Kingdom, by helping God's people learn to understand the real and only truth, which are the living words of God. I also feel that God has giving me a divine gift in this calling to do this through writing books and speaking to His people. Since God has giving me this divine Gift, I will always give all the glory to Him in the highest. I give praise to His almighty name above all names, the Alpha and the Omega, who was, who is and who is to come.

Revelation 1:8 *"I am the Alpha and the Omega," says the Lord God, "who is, and who was, and who is to come, the Almighty."*

I am also so very grateful that Jesus my Lord and Savior had such a deep unconditional loving passion to redeem me and you all from the curse Satan had on us all and Jesus did so with such a relentless conviction to finish the will of His Father. Praise to the King of Kings and Lord of Lords. My Redeemer lives!

Revelation 19:16 *On his robe and on his thigh he has this name written: KING OF KINGS AND LORD OF LORDS.*

Job 19:25 *I know that my Redeemer lives, and that in the end he will stand upon the earth.*

"The most important thing that God has given us all is His divine gift of unconditional love. Without that love, everything that God has created would cease to exist. Everything hangs on that love, because God is love.

~Michael Anthony Gagliardi~

True wisdom is when you know and understand that you are nothing without the Lord in your life.

~Michael Anthony Gagliardi~

And in knowing and understanding that you are nothing without the Lord in your life, makes you one of the smartest.

~Michael Anthony Gagliardi~

Table of Contents

A Divine Connection
With A Message From God

Volume II

"Michael!" Yes Lord.
"You Have Been Redeemed!"

Introduction

Psalm 107:2 *Let the redeemed of the LORD tell their story— those he redeemed from the hand of the foe,*

This book series A Divine Connection With A Message From God Volume II subtitle "Michael!" Yes Lord. "You Have Been Redeemed!" You will learn and discover the real meaning of what it truly means to be redeemed by God at the cross at Calvary. I will also walk you through several of what I truly believe were real personal divine connections with God in Heaven when He spoke to me about Him redeeming me and about my walk and talk with Jesus here on earth and how He healed me before He had to return Back to Heaven to again return.

Why God chose me to reveal this certain things to me, I don't fully know. Maybe because my heart mind and soul were and is open to receive it or maybe I guess He knows that I will do something with it, according to His will in Christ Jesus. I truly feel that the Holy Spirit wants me to share it with as many people as possible before His second coming.

Well, during the reading of this particular book series volume II, you will also learn and discover how the precious shed blood of Jesus at the cross at Calvary has and will continue to give you victory over any and every situation you face here on Earth, until you enter the Kingdom of Heaven.

I feel most Christian people don't really get that real divine connection with God and might never really fully understand what He truly did for us at the cross at Calvary by Him redeeming us and I fully understand why. I truly believe it's because, once they got born again in Christ Jesus, most Christians failed to want and continue to have a real personal relationship with Him by continuing to pray and meditate on His living words daily.

I truly believe that if you ask most people, who is Jesus to them or what did he do for them? Most would probably say "Well, he died for my all my sins, so I could go to Heaven." Well, that's true, but there is much more that their missing here. I also truly believe that they would probably tell you that with not to much emotion in their statement and I fully understand why. It's because they don't know Him on a personal level and don't feel that close to Him. Just like if you heard of someone passing away you didn't really know that well and you were not that close with, you probably wouldn't be as emotional to their death as you would be for someone very close to and know personally, right? I hope you said right.

When I see people walking around sad, worry, stress out, depressed and just plain unhappy, I know for a fact that they don't have that real personal relationship with Jesus, because if they truly did, they would know, not assume, how to get into a rejoicing mood and to change their circumstance through Christ Jesus.

Philippians 4:4 *Rejoice in the Lord always. I will say it again: Rejoice!*

If nothing else, God's people should be walking around with complete amazement that their hopefully not going to hell if they died, but are going to Heaven to be with God the father in eternal glory. Praise the Lord! Get all excited!

Psalm 118:17 *I will not die but live, and will proclaim what the LORD has done.*

You should give Him praise everyday for what He has done for all of us who accepted Him as our Lord and Savior. Our Redeemer lives! Get to know Him! Get all excited and tell everybody that Jesus Christ is King and our Redeemer lives! Praise His mighty name above all names! The King of Kings and Lord of Lords! The great I Am! The Alpha and the Omega! The First and Last!

The Beginning and End! Praise the Lord our Redeemer lives!

Job 19:25 *I know that my Redeemer lives, and that in the end he will stand upon the earth.*

All I can tell you is this; you will never fully know and understand how to have God's real true joy, true peace, true love and true happiness, unless you surrender completely and unconditionally to Him and His living words. Once you do that start renewing your mind with constant meditation on His living words day and night and constant prayer. It's never too late to get started. So what are you waiting for?

Romans 12:2 (KJV) *And be not conformed to this world: but be ye transformed by the renewing of your mind, that ye may prove what is that good, and acceptable, and perfect, will of God.*

Chapter 1

"Michael!" Yes Lord. "You Have Been Redeemed!"

Acts 2:17 (NIV) *In the last days, God says, I will pour out my Spirit on all people. Your sons and daughters will prophesy, your young men will see visions, your old men will dream dreams.*

This Bible verse has came so real and alive to me many times in my life when I had so many dreams where God has spoken to me, talked with me, walked with me, healed me and showed me visions of His second coming.

I remember a past dream when I opened my spiritual eyes in the dream and I was in someone's house. When I look around to see where I was, I saw my mother and my older brother was there also. I could not see there physical faces, but somehow I just knew it was them. I realized later after the dream I was seeing their spirits. They told me that I was in Heaven and boy I was in awe.

During the time this was happening to me, I didn't really realize that I was dreaming this. They began to explain things to me and showing me around their beautiful house in Heaven, because I guess somehow they new that I just arrived and everything was so new to me there and I had a lot of questions to ask them just about everything that was going on. I could see that they were so excited that I was there with them in Heaven.

John 14:2 (KJV) *In my Father's house are many mansions: if it were not so, I would have told you. I go to prepare a place for you.?*

While we were spending time together in the house, I heard loud noises coming from outside the house, so I then looked out the window to see where it was all coming from. It was coming from what appeared to be the center of Heaven and there were very large crowds of people there, I would say many thousands of them. I then realized they were standing around the throne of God and where all worshiping God who sat on His throne.

Revelation 14:3 (NIV) *And they sang a new song before the throne and before the four living creatures and the elders. No one could learn the song except the 144,000 who had been redeemed from the earth.*

I then remembered that, I wanted to go down there to check it out, so I went down towards the crowd and began to walk in the mist of them. With so many people there, I figure that God wouldn't notice me right away with all the noise and so many people there worshiping. Boy, I was wrong.

While watching everything that was going on walking in the mist of the crowds, the presence of Almighty God came upon me so fast and it was like I was the only one there in the crowd. It was like no one else was now there. It was also like His presence extended toward me all the way from His throne with such mighty power like the mightiest wind. I then immediately remember falling to the ground with such shame from all I have sins while on earth.

The next thing I heard was the mighty voice of God, which was like greater than any earthly thunder I have ever heard on earth. He then said to me, "Adulterer! You Have Been Redeemed!" His voice was so powerful, that I immediately woke up from the dream. The dream was so profound to me that I couldn't go back to sleep. I realized that I couldn't hide anything from God, He knows everything.

Isaiah 44 (NIV) *I have swept away your offenses like a cloud, your sins like the morning mist. Return to me, for I have redeemed you.*"

Since that day, I began to fully understand what Jesus really did for all of us at the cross at Calvary. All my life after I was born again at an early age, I knew that Jesus died for my sins and rose again by God the Father, but I thought I knew what that really meant. Since that dream and divine connection with God I realized that I didn't have a close personal relationship with Him and I was not being totally grateful for what He did for me at the cross at Calvary. I guess when your not that close to someone, you don't get that emotionally involve in that person and your feelings of that person are so far away that anything won't stir you up inside like someone that is close to you.

I also began to then realize that I was purchased for a price, which I didn't have to even pay back. I was also purchased for a price, which I didn't even deserve. I was also purchased for a price, which I didn't even have to ask for or even beg for. I was also purchased for a price out of unconditional love when I didn't even deserve to be loved. I was also purchased for a price when I was guilty and I deserved to be punished for it. I was also purchased from death, hell and the grave, so I could eventually live in eternal glory with God the Father in Heaven. Praise the Lord! Praise the Lord! Praise the Lord! If that alone don't get you excited everyday you need to start meditating on the living words of God more and pray more to get a closer personal relationship with Him.

Luke 1:68 (NIV) *Praise be to the Lord, the God of Israel, because he has come to his people and redeemed them.*

Lamentations 3:58 (NIV) *You, Lord, took up my case; you redeemed my life.*

I also realized that there is nothing in this world good I could have done or do to deserve being redeemed (purchased for a price) by Jesus at the cross at Calvary. It was by His mercy and grace He redeemed me by shedding His precious blood at the cross at Calvary, which broke the curse that Satan caused, when Adam and Eve in the beginning were deceived by Satan and disobeyed God's law in the Garden of Eden. By Jesus breaking this curse for us, it allowed us full access to God the father though Him. It also allows us to have complete authority, power and protection over Satan and his evil tricks, sickness, disease and everything and anything that could come against us here on earth, until we enter the Kingdom of Heaven.

Galatians 3:13 *Christ redeemed us from the curse of the law by becoming a curse for us, for it is written: "Cursed is everyone who is hung on a pole."*

Revelation 22:3 *No longer will there be any curse. The throne of God and of the Lamb will be in the city, and his servants will serve him.*

Now that you know what God did for you at the cross at Calvary, you should want to serve and honor Him with all your heart, mind, body and soul. He paid the price for you and me. Honor and Serve Him! Praise His all mighty name above all names. He is our King of Kings and Lord of Lords. He is our creator of the universe. He is the Alpha and Omega. He is the Beginning and the End. He is the First and the Last. He was, He is and is to come.

Our Redeemer Lives! Praise the Lord! Give Him praise! Amen.

1 Corinthians 6:20 (NIV) *you were bought at a price. Therefore honor God with your bodies*

If you still can't really grasp what Jesus did for you and me at the cross at Calvary by shedding His blood for all of our sins and breaking the curse of Satan, here is a great illustration I heard by Dr. Creflo Dollar, while watching one of his great TV sermons recently on the power of the blood of Jesus.

There was a slave girl who was being sold at an auction block to the highest bidder to be owned again as a slave by another master. When it was her time to be sold, she was put on the auction block and the bidding for her began. As the new potential masters were bidding, the bids began to go up higher and higher as the new potential masters wanted to buy her as a slave for themselves. The bids began to get so high for the slave girl that most of these new potential masters stop bidding except for a few, because they would not and could not afford to lose anymore just for a slave girl.

However, there was this one new potential master bidding that was so relentless in his bidding that he was not stopping, until he won the bid for the slave girl. After the bids got higher and higher for the slave girl, everyone stopped bidding except this one new master and he finally won the bid for this slave girl. He paid the highest price that anyone would or could ever pay for just a slave girl.

After he paid the price and went to redeem the slave girl, the auction people brought the slave girl to the new master who had paid for her with such a high price that everyone still could not believe. The new owner had the slave girl sit down in front of him and handed her some papers stating to her, "I just want you to know I would have gave everything to purchase and redeem you and nothing would have stop me. Here is your papers giving you back your freedom, you are free to go and you are no longer a slave to anyone anymore."

When the girl heard and saw what her new master did for her, she got on her knees and began to cry asking her new master why he would do this for her. Her master said to her, "It's because I love you more than you can ever know and you are so priceless to me that I would do anything and everything within my power to save you from slavery."

When the girl heard that, she had tears in her eyes realizing she had been set free. She began rejoicing that now she would have true peace, true joy, true love and true happiness. She then told her new master that, since he did that for her, she would honor and serve him forever.

I hope after you read this awesome illustration of redemption, you get some understanding of what Jesus did for you and us all at the cross at Calvary and the sacrifice Jesus went through by becoming the true Lamb of God shedding His blood, so that you and I would be set free from being a slave to sin and all that is associated with sin. I'm telling you the truth; once you know the real and only truth (The living words of God) the truth will set you free. Once the Son (Jesus) sets you free, you will be free indeed. Amen

John 8:31-36 *[31] To the Jews who had believed him, Jesus said, "If you hold to my teaching, you are really my disciples. [32] Then you will know the truth, and the truth will set you free." [33] They answered him, "We are Abraham's descendants and have never been slaves of anyone. How can you say that we shall be set free?" [34] Jesus replied, "I tell you the truth, everyone who sins is a slave to sin. [35] Now a slave has no permanent place in the family, but a son belongs to it forever. [36] So if the Son sets you free, you will be free indeed.*

Chapter 2

I saw Jesus coming down from in the Clouds Above

Deuteronomy 33:26 *There is no one like the God of Jeshurun, who rides across the heavens to help you and on the clouds in his majesty.*

Another divine connection I had with the Lord is when I had a dream and when I look up in the sky with my spiritual eyes, I saw Jesus walking on the clouds. At first I taught it was just my imagination, so I looked up again and saw Jesus coming down from the clouds towards me. I was so excited like a child in a toy store singing and rejoicing watching Him coming down from the clouds to touch down next to me.

Psalm 68:4 *Sing to God, sing in praise of his name, extol him who rides on the clouds; rejoice before him— his name is the LORD.*

Job 35:5 *Look up at the heavens and see; gaze at the clouds so high above you.*

Job 37:15 *Do you know how God controls the clouds and makes his lightning flash?*

Psalm 18:9 *He parted the heavens and came down; dark clouds were under his feet.*

Matthew 5:8 *Blessed are the pure in heart, for they will see God.*

With what appeared to be a moment of a few seconds, Jesus was standing right next to me looking at me. I remember yelling to everyone with such a true peace, true joy, true love and true happiness that Jesus was here with me. It was so awesome and I felt like a little kid again, yet I was about 25 years old. I remember just looking at His face in awe. His eyes were so beautiful and piercing and He stood there for a moment just looking at me. I felt so much comfort and secure next to him as He stood there with a smile on His face as He stared at me.

Matthew 6:8 *Your Father knows what you need before you ask him.*

As I look at Him staring at me, I just started thinking about everything I wanted to ask Him. It was so neat. He knew my every thought even before I ask or even before I thought of something. We were communicating not with our mouths, but with our spirits. I really didn't have to talk or ask Him anything with my mouth, because He already knew everything and He knew everything I needed. It was so unbelievable. We began just hanging out together walking and talking and just having so much fun like little children in a play ground.

Matthew 18:3 *And he said: "Truly I tell you, unless you change and become like little children, you will never enter the kingdom of heaven.*

After a while I guess the playing around was over and I realized He came for a purpose. He came to heal me from all my afflictions I was facing at that time in my life. I began to try and tell Him again what was going on with me, but again He already knew and told me to be still.

Psalm 46:10 *He says, "Be still, and know that I am God; I will be exalted among the nations, I will be exalted in the earth."*

He knew everything about me, even more than I thought I knew. Let face it, He's God. The Question is, can anyone teach God Knowledge? The answer is a big NO, since He is The Creator of the Universe, the Alpha and Omega, our high Priest, the King of Kings and the Lord of Lords and He judges even the highest.

Job 21:22 *Can anyone teach knowledge to God, since he judges even the highest?*

He then began to touch me with his mighty right hand where I needed to be healed on my body. Every time He touched me, I felt the power of what His mighty right hand had in it that went straight through my entire body. It was like a strong energy field going through my entire body like I was a battery being recharged or something. I just knew when it was happening; I was being made whole again.

Psalm 30:2 *LORD my God, I called to you for help, and you healed me.*

Revelation 21:5 *"I am making everything new!"*

After He was finished healing me, I then began to show Him all of my physical scars I had on my body. He knew already, again He's God. He took His right index finger and went over all of my scars I had on my body. It was like His right finger was welding the scars back together. Every time He ran His right finger over my scars, it left like what appeared to be a scab or something. All I can tell you is that, His right finger had so much mighty power in it. When I went to touch the scabs after He touched them, He stopped me and told me, "Do not touch them right away, let them heal first." So I left them alone. I think that He was telling me that all scars physical and spiritually will eventually heal, if we just leave them alone and stop picking at them, which will delay the healing process. The final thing He did to me was that, He took His right index finger again and touched the center of my chest with it. Again I felt His mighty power going straight through me. I now believe today that when He did that, He restored me as new and burned His living words into the walls of my heart, mind and soul.

Job 33:25 *let their flesh be renewed like a child's; let them be restored as in the days of their youth*

After healing me He told me He had to go for now and would be back soon. It was so awesome watching Him leave. He spread out His hands and started going back up in the air into the clouds and back to Heaven. As I watched Him go higher and higher in the sky, I remember yelling to Him to stop for a moment. It was awesome He heard me and stop in mid air and hovered there to listen to me. I then ask Him to say hello to the Father for me. He then smile and nodded his head that he would and continued going back up.

Psalm 104:3 *and lays the beams of his upper chambers on their waters. He makes the clouds his chariot and rides on the wings of the wind.*

When I woke up from the dream, I could still feel His finger on my chest. Wow! That was such an awesome divine connection with a message from God. Even today 20 years later, it still fills like yesterday that I walked, talked and was healed by Jesus, my best friend, my comforter, my Lord, my Savior and my everlasting redeemer, who was, who is and is to come as our King of Kings and Lord of Lords. Praise the Lord!

Chapter 3

God's Almighty Power, Protection & Authority That Is in the Precious Blood of the Lamb Jesus Christ

Exodus 12:1-13 *[1] The LORD said to Moses and Aaron in Egypt, [2] "This month is to be for you the first month, the first month of your year. [3] Tell the whole community of Israel that on the tenth day of this month each man is to take a lamb for his family, one for each household. [4] If any household is too small for a whole lamb, they must share one with their nearest neighbor, having taken into account the number of people there are. You are to determine the amount of lamb needed in accordance with what each person will eat. [5] The animals you choose must be year-old males without defect, and you may take them from the sheep or the goats. [6] Take care of them until the fourteenth day of the month, when all the members of the community of Israel must slaughter them at twilight. [7]*

Then they are to take some of the blood and put it on the sides and tops of the doorframes of the houses where they eat the lambs. [8] That same night they are to eat the meat roasted over the fire, along with bitter herbs, and bread made without yeast. [9] Do not eat the meat raw or boiled in water, but roast it over a fire—with the head, legs and internal organs. [10] Do not leave any of it till morning; if some is left till morning, you must burn it. [11] This is how you are to eat it: with your cloak tucked into your belt, your sandals on your feet and your staff in your hand. Eat it in haste; it is the LORD's Passover.

[12] *"On that same night I will pass through Egypt and strike down every firstborn of both people and animals, and I will bring judgment on all the gods of Egypt. I am the LORD. [13] The blood will be a sign for you on the houses where you are, and when I see the blood, I will pass over you. No destructive plague will touch you when I strike Egypt.*

We see in the living words of God in the above Bible scriptures, that there is much power in the blood of a lamb, when God commanded His people to sacrifice it and put the blood of lamb on the sides and tops of their doorframes of their houses. They were also commanded to eat of the entire lamb before morning. God promised them that, if they obey all His commandments on that day, He would Passover their homes and be protected, when the wrath of God went through Egypt to strike down every firstborn of both people and animals to bring judgment on all the gods of Egypt.

When God commanded them to eat the entire lamb before morning, it is my belief that, this was a symbol for them that God wanted them to have all the properties of the sacrificed lamb to become alive inside them to cover their sins when He Passover their houses where the blood of the lamb was on their door frames. That symbolic symbol represents what the same thing we must do when you invite Jesus (the true Lamb of God) to come and live inside us as our Lord and Savior who sanctifies you, to become righteous in the eyes of the Father. It is also my belief that God was observing their obedience to all of His commandments that day He gave them during His Passover, so they would remain holy and covered by the blood of the lamb.

1 Peter 1:19 *but with the precious blood of Christ, a lamb without blemish or defect.*

Matthew 26:28 *This is my blood of the covenant, which is poured out for many for the forgiveness of sins.*

Now just think for a moment, this was animal blood that had the power to cover their sins and save them from the strike of God's wrath, when He brought judgment on all the gods of Egypt. Now how much more power, protection and authority that we have in the blood of the living Lamb of God (Jesus), which did not just covers us from sin, but it sanctified us from sin whiter than snow and it also broke the curse of Satan, which gave us full authority, power and protection over Satan, so we can live our lives here on earth with complete victory. When we are covered with the blood of the Lamb of God (Jesus), all the properties of Him are in us, which means we have the God's Power, authority and Protection in us. It reminds me of the song we use to sing in church when I was little boy. "There is Power, Power, wonder working Power in the precious blood of the Lamb. There is Power, Power, wonder working Power in the precious blood of the Lamb." Praise His Mighty Name!

John 14:12 *Very truly I tell you, whoever believes in me will do the works I have been doing, and they will do even greater things than these, because I am going to the Father.*

Just like when God's people in Egypt had the animal lamb inside them by them eating it, we now have the true precious Lamb of God (Jesus) in us and all of His properties (His righteousness, power, protection and authority over Satan's army, death, hell and the grave), which is life and we can have it now more abundantly.

Matthew 16:19 *I will give you the keys of the kingdom of heaven; whatever you bind on earth will be bound in heaven, and whatever you loose on earth will be loosed in heaven."*

John 10:10 (KJV) *The thief cometh not, but for to steal, and to kill, and to destroy: I am come that they might have life, and that they might have it more abundantly.*

Here is a great illustration on how Jesus and all of his power are transferred in us. Think of Jesus as a powerful magnet and you a piece of steel. When the steel get closer to the magnet, they are drawn together with a mighty force. Like when you ask Jesus to come and live in your heart as your Lord and Savior.

Now what is unique about the magnet and steel is that, once the steel gets connected to the magnet, it too becomes magnetized like the magnet. All the properties in the magnet get transferred to the steel, like when you ask Jesus to come and live in your heart as your Lord and Savior, all of His properties get transferred inside you. Even if you separate magnet and steel, the steel still remains magnetized, because it still retains some of the properties of the magnet, just like if you try to separate from God, you still have properties of Him in you. Our bodies are His when we accept him in our hearts. Praise the Lord!

1 Corinthians 6:19 *Do you not know that your bodies are temples of the Holy Spirit, who is in you, whom you have received from God? You are not your own*

Now the more we meditate on the living words of God and get closer to Him, we get more magnetized with Him, which give us more power (more trust, faith and belief in His living words). The more powerful the magnet, the more powerful force it has. The more you trust and have the faith to believe in God's living words, the more powerful force you have in Christ Jesus and

Christ Jesus in you. Now how big of a magnet do you want to become with the living words of God? It your choice, your decision, I say choose wisely. Surrender totally unconditionally to God and His living words with constant meditation and prayer. Become a huge powerful magnet in Christ Jesus today and forever, so you can live a life with total victory here on earth, until you enter the Kingdom of Heaven.

Joshua 1:8 *Do not let this Book of the Law depart from your mouth; meditate on it day and night, so that you may be careful to do everything written in it. Then you will be prosperous and successful.*

1 John 4:4 (KJV) *Greater is he that is in you, than he that is in the world.*

Philippians 4:13 (KJV) *I can do all things through Christ which strengtheneth me.*

Romans 8:31 *If God is for us, who can be against us?*

Isaiah 54:17 (Amplified Bible) *But no weapon that is formed against you shall prosper*

Chapter 4

You Have an Invisible Force Field of Protection with God's Almighty Power, Protection & Authority That Is in the Precious Blood of the Lamb Jesus Christ

1 Corinthians 6:19 *Do you not know that your bodies are temples of the Holy Spirit, who is in you, whom you have received from God? You are not your own.*

When you know and understand that the almighty God lives inside you through His Holy spirit is like you having an invisible force field of power and protection that you cannot see with your physical eyes, but Satan and his demons can see it and they know they can not penetrate through it, unless you allow them too. Demons shudder just by the name of God. They know Him who was, who is and is to come, the almighty God. Praise the Lord!

James 2:19 *You believe that there is one God. Good! Even the demons believe that and shudder.*

John 14:17 (Amplified Bible) *The Spirit of Truth, Whom the world cannot receive (welcome, take to its heart), because it does not see Him or know and recognize Him. But you know and recognize Him, for He lives with you [constantly] and will be in you.*

Satan and his many demons always will have a deep evil passion and a constant relentless conviction to try to get through your invisible force field of God's power and protection that surrounds you, by trying to destroy you from the inside out.

Satan and his many demons will do this by attacking your mind (your control center), by always trying to get your complete focus off of God and His living words, so that your trust, faith and belief in Him and His living words will become weaken enough that they can begin their attack on you.

Satan and his many demons know that this is the only way that your God invisible force field of power and protection that surrounds you will weaken enough where they can begin to penetrate it, to begin to try and destroy you from the inside out.

1 John 5: 18-20 *[18]We know that anyone born of God does not continue to sin; the one who was born of God keeps him safe, and the evil one cannot harm him. [19]We know that we are children of God, and that the whole world is under the control of the evil one. [20]We know also that the Son of God has come and has given us understanding, so that we may know him who is true. And we are in him who is true—even in his Son Jesus Christ. He is the true God and eternal life.*

Also don't think for one minute that Satan and his demons don't know and understand how this invisible force field of God's power and protection works that surrounds you through the Holy Spirit. Satan and his many demons know exactly how your mind (your control center) operates and he will do anything and everything in his power to try to gain control of your mind (your thoughts), if you allow him to do so.

1 Timothy 4:1 *The Spirit clearly says that in later times some will abandon the faith and follow deceiving spirits and things taught by demons.*

Also it is our own doing that permits Satan and his demons spirits to enter into our lives. God does not cause evil, but He will allow it in our lives, if we allow our self to permit it in by our lack of knowledge and understanding of God's living words.

Hosea 4:6 *my people are destroyed from lack of knowledge. "Because you have rejected knowledge, I also reject you as my priests; because you have ignored the law of your God, I also will ignore your children.*

God gives us full authority of His almighty power & protection over Satan and his demons through the Holy Spirit that is in us, which we are certified, stamped and covered by the precious blood of the Lamb Jesus Christ.

Matthew 16:19 *I will give you the keys of the kingdom of heaven; whatever you bind on earth will be bound in heaven, and whatever you loose on earth will be loosed in heaven."*

Deuteronomy 30:19 *This day I call heaven and earth as witnesses against you that I have set before you life and death, blessings and curses. Now choose life, so that you and your children may live.*

Proverbs 18:21 *The tongue has the power of life and death and those who love it will eat its fruit.*

2 Thessalonians 3:3 *But the Lord is faithful, and he will strengthen and protect you from the evil one.*

1 John 4:4 (KJV) *Greater is he that is in you, than he that is in the world.*

Philippians 4:13 (KJV) *I can do all things through Christ which strengtheneth me.*

Romans 8:31 *If God is for us, who can be against us?*

Isaiah 41:10 (Amplified Bible) *Fear not [there is nothing to fear], for I am with you; do not look around you in terror and be dismayed, for I am your God. I will strengthen and harden you to difficulties, yes, I will help you; yes, I will hold you up and retain you with My [victorious] right hand of rightness and justice.*

Psalm 18:2 *The LORD is my rock, my fortress and my deliverer; my God is my rock, in whom I take refuge. He is my shield and the horn of my salvation, my stronghold.*

Satan wants you to get so far away from knowing, understanding, trusting and having the faith to believe the real and only truth (the living words of God), so that you will become so alone and lost in a forest of lies, with no hope of even getting out or knowing what to do to get out.

Satan and his evil army had and still have a deep evil passion and a relentless conviction to try to destroy everything God has created, but they have no power to defeat God. However, Satan is skilled at lying and convincing people to listen to his lies, because he knows his time is short and that is the only weapon he has. So be very strong and continue to keep your focus on God and His living words with a deep loving passion and a relentless conviction to keep 100% trust, faith and belief in God and His living words.

1 Peter 5:8-9 *Be self-controlled and alert. Your enemy the devil prowls around like a roaring lion looking for*

someone to devour. ⁹Resist him, standing firm in the faith, because you know that your brothers throughout the world are undergoing the same kind of sufferings.

Here is an illustration on how this force field of God's protection operates on your life and how Satan can weaken it or even destroy it to finish the job.

I am a real movie buff and I like just about anything especially when there is a real good meaningful ending to it. When I watched Independents' Day with actor Will Smith in it among many others, I notice something in the movie that really showed me how Satan tries to destroy us. If you saw the movie great, if not, I will do my best to explain it to you the best I can.

In the movie alien spaceships came to earth and began to position themselves all over the world to try to destroy all of man kind on the planet. While all the alien spaceships were getting into their position to strike us all at the same time, we and the rest of the world tried to stop them by attacking them with massive military force, but could not penetrate their spaceships, because they had an invisible force field of protection that surrounded each of their spaceships.

Well, there was one man who figured out how to destroy the spaceships. He realized that the force field they could not penetrate was coming from the command center on the alien's mother spaceship in outer space. He figured out that if he could somehow insert a destructive computer virus into the alien's mother spaceship command center, then all the other spaceships on earth would lose their protected force fields and then we could attack them and destroy them all.

Well, to do that, they needed to get through the alien's mother spaceship protected force field first, so they could plant the destructive computer virus. So they decided to use an alien spaceship that had crashed on earth many years before that they had kept a secret from the entire world. Since the alien's mother spaceship arrived, the alien spaceship they had kept secret started working again. So they figured they would use it to get permission to enter into the alien's mother spaceship to plant the destructive computer virus.

Well, their plan worked and they were able to enter to plant the destructive computer virus. While inside the alien's mother spaceship, they planted the virus and we attack them when their protected force fields on all the alien spaceships went down and they were all destroyed. The people, who planted the virus on the alien's mother spaceship, engaged a timed bomb on it before they left it to go back to earth, which completely destroy it.

What is so unique about this movie is that Satan knows and understands already that your mind (your control center) works like the alien's mother spaceship in the movie, which controls God's protected force field that surrounds you. Satan will use everything and anything possible to try somehow to gain access into your mind to try to destroy you from the inside out. Satan will even disguise himself as good to get permission to enter your mind, than once he is in, he will try to destroy you from the inside out. That is the only way he can try to harm or destroy you.

Jesus warns us to watch out for false prophets that come in sheep's clothing, but inwardly they are ferocious wolves. God said, *"By their fruit you will recognize them"* That's why it's so important to know and understand God's living words and not assume it, but know it!

Matthew 7:15-16 *[15] "Watch out for false prophets. They come to you in sheep's clothing, but inwardly they are ferocious wolves. [16] By their fruit you will recognize them. Do people pick grapes from thorn bushes, or figs from thistles?*

We are not fighting against flesh and blood, but against the rulers, authorities, powers of the dark world and the spiritual forces of evil in the heavenly realms. We should be strong in the Lord and in his mighty power, by putting on the full armor of God, so that we can take our stand against the devil's schemes.

By putting on the full armor of God, the living words of God declares that, we should pray in the spirit on all occasions with all kinds of prayers and requests. And with this in mind, we must be alert and always keep praying for all the saints. Pray and continuously pray.

Ephesians 6:10-18 *[10]Finally, be strong in the Lord and in his mighty power. [11]Put on the full armor of God so that you can take your stand against the devil's schemes. [12]For our struggle is not against flesh and blood, but against the rulers, against the authorities, against the powers of this dark world and against the spiritual forces of evil in the heavenly realms. [13]Therefore put on the full armor of God, so that when the day of evil comes, you may be able to stand your ground, and after you have done everything, to stand. [14]Stand firm then, with the belt of truth buckled around your waist, with the breastplate of righteousness in place, [15]and with your feet fitted with the readiness that comes from the gospel of peace. [16]In addition to all this, take up the shield of faith, with which you can extinguish all the flaming arrows of the evil one. [17]Take the helmet of salvation and the sword of the Spirit, which is the word of God. [18]And pray in the Spirit on all occasions with all kinds of prayers and requests. With this in mind, be alert and always keep on praying for all the saints.*

58

Chapter 5

Start Use~ing~ the ~ING~ in Your Life to Fully Activate God's Almighty Power, Protection & Authority That Is in the Precious Blood of the Lamb Jesus Christ

Let me start from the begin~ing~.

John 1:1 *In the beginning was the Word, and the Word was with God, and the Word was God.*

The First ~ING~ factor that you should use to fully activate the almighty power and protection in the precious blood of the Lamb (Jesus Christ) is to start by create~ing~ your eternal everlast~ing~ future in Christ Jesus by ask~ing~ Him to come and live in your heart as your Lord and Savior, because He is the only way, the truth and the life. No one goes to the Father in Heaven except through Him. Jesus didn't say that there was a way; He said He was the way, which means there is no other way, but through Him only.

John 14:6 *Jesus answered, "I am the way and the truth and the life. No one comes to the Father except through me.*

The next ~ING~ factor that you should use to fully activate the almighty power in the precious blood of the Lamb (Jesus Christ) is by believe~ing~, that Jesus is truly God the Father's only begotten Son, so you will not perish, but have eternal everlast~ing~ life.

John 3:16 (KJV) *[16]For God so loved the world, that he gave his only begotten Son, that whosoever believeth in him should not perish, but have everlasting life.*

The next ~ING~ factor that you should use to fully activate the almighty power in the precious blood of the Lamb (Jesus Christ) is by confess~ing~ with your mouth the Lord Jesus and again by believe~ing~ in your heart that God the Father raised Him from the dead, you will be saved by God deliver~ing~ you from the curse of Satan, which is the fear of death, hell and the grave. Also what you need to do is start by the confess~ing~ of all your sins, for He is faithful to forgive us and purify us whiter than snow from all unrighteousness.

Romans 10:9 (KJV) *That if thou shalt confess with thy mouth the Lord Jesus, and shalt believe in thine heart that God hath raised him from the dead, thou shalt be saved.*

John 1:9 *If we confess our sins, he is faithful and just and will forgive us our sins and purify us from all unrighteousness.*

The next ~ING~ factor you should use to fully activate the almighty power in the precious blood of the Lamb (Jesus Christ) is by repent~ing~ and by baptize~ing~ in the name of Jesus Christ for Him forgive~ing~ you of all your sins, so that we will have the gift of the Holy Spirit by Receive~ing ~ it from God.

Acts 2:38 *Peter replied, "Repent and be baptized, every one of you, in the name of Jesus Christ for the forgiveness of your sins. And you will receive the gift of the Holy Spirit.*

Now if you decided to follow the above mentioned ~ING~ factors, you're now in the body of Christ Jesus.

The next ~ING factor you should use to fully activate the almighty power in the precious blood of the Lamb (Jesus Christ) is to begin by follow~ing~, honor~ing~ and serve~ing~ Him by acknowledge~ing~ Him daily in all your ways, which then you will be able to start by dedicate~ing~ your life to Him completely by totally surrender~ing~ unconditionally to Him and His live~ing~ words daily moment by moment.

Once you do this you will be able to start to begin by trust~ing~ God more and have~ing~ the faith in believe~ing~ in Him and His live~ing~ words.

Proverbs 3:5-6 *⁵ Trust in the LORD with all your heart and lean not on your own understanding; in all your ways acknowledge him, and he will make your paths straight.*

Once you make that choice, that decision to fully activate God's almighty power, protection and authority, which is in the precious blood of the Lamb (Jesus Christ), you need to start by study~ing~, meditate~ing~ and Learn~ing~ the live~ing~ words of God day and night, so you can begin by know~ing~ and understand~ing~ it and you can do so by read~ing~, listen~ing~, hear~ing~, see~ing~, speak~ing~, forgiv~ing~, fast~ing~, thank~ing~, praise~ing~ and worship~ing~, sing~ing~, love~ing~, rejoice~ing~, dance~ing~, shout~ing~, cry~ing~ and then by comunicate~ing~ to Him through pray~ing~ constantly.

Joshua 1:8 *Do not let this Book of the Law depart from your mouth; meditate on it day and night, so that you may be careful to do everything written in it. Then you will be prosperous and successful.*

2 Thessalonians 3:2 *And pray that we may be delivered from wicked and evil men, for not everyone has faith.*

Proverbs 2:6 *For the LORD gives wisdom, and from his mouth come knowledge and understanding.*

Psalm 119:73 *Your hands made me and formed me; give me understanding to learn your commands.*

Psalm 5:11 *But let all who take refuge in you be glad; let them ever sing for joy. Spread your protection over them, that those who love your name may rejoice in you.*

Matthew 4:40 *Jesus answered, "It is written: 'Man does not live on bread alone, but on every word that comes from the mouth of God.'*

Psalm 25:5 *Guide me in your truth and teach me, for you are God my Savior, and my hope is in you all day long.*

Hosea 4:6 *My people are destroyed from lack of knowledge. "Because you have rejected knowledge, I also reject you as my priests; because you have ignored the law of your God, I also will ignore your children.*

Once you do this you will start know~ing~ God's wisdom and understand~ing~ of the real and only truth, the live~ing~ words of God.

By do~ing~ this if your still will~ing~ to continue follow~ing~ Him and continue surrender~ing~ to Him on a daily basic moment by moment, God will begin teach~ing~ and change~ing~ you through His Holy Spirit, so that you will not be destroyed from lack of knowledge, but become very prosperous and successful in every area of your life.

Once again if you continue do this faithfully, you will begin by love~ing and trust~ing~ God more each day and you will start to begin by have~ing~ the faith in believe~ing~ in Him and His live~ing~ words.

How can you not trust in someone you love so much for what He did for you at the cross at Calvary by shed~ing~ His precious blood for you? You Can't! When you love someone with so much love~ing~ passion, you can't help to trust in that person with all your heart, mind and soul. That's why it is so important to get to really know God on a personal level and have a real personal relationship with Him,

Jesus even teaches us in the Bible that God's Greatest Commandment is to love the Lord your God with all your heart and with all your soul and with all entire mind. And the second is like it. Love your neighbor as yourself. God even goes on to say that, without these two laws, nothing in His live~ing~ words would function.

Matthew 22 36-40 The Greatest Commandment
³⁶"Teacher, which is the greatest commandment in the

Law?" ³⁷Jesus replied: " 'Love the Lord your God with all your heart and with all your soul and with all entire mind.' ³⁸This is the first and greatest commandment. ³⁹And the second is like it: 'Love your neighbor as yourself.' ⁴⁰All the Law and the Prophets hang on these two commandments."

1 John 4:8 (KJV) *He that loveth not knoweth not God; for God is love.*

Stop conform~ing~ to this world anymore, but keep on transform~ing~ yourself by renew~ing~ your mind through eat~ing~ and meditate~ing~ on the words of God, so then you will begin to start by love~ing~ and trust~ing~ God more and then have~ing~ the faith in believe~ing~ in Him and His live~ing~ words. This will satisfied all your hunger and thirst all of the time.

Romans 12:2 (KJV) *And be not conformed to this world: but be ye transformed by the renewing of your mind, that ye may prove what is that good, and acceptable, and perfect, will of God.*

John 6:35 *Then Jesus declared, "I am the bread of life. He who comes to me will never go hungry, and he who believes in me will never be thirsty."*

As you continue to do this, you can then begin to start by live~ing~ your life with true peace, true joy, true love and true happiness more abundantly here on earth, until you enter the Kingdom of Heaven.

John 10:10 (KJV) *The thief cometh not, but for to steal, and to kill, and to destroy: I am come that they might have life, and that they might have it more abundantly.*

God already knows and understands the ~ING~ factor in the power of His Son's precious Blood that was shed at the cross at Calvary. He knows that His Son's precious blood can be protect~ing~ us by shield~ing~ us all from any harm and by heal~ing~ us all from any sickness or disease and also by deliver~ing~ us from any and all troubles that we might face here on earth, until we all enter the Kingdom of Heaven.

Psalm 32:7 *You are my hiding place; you will protect me from trouble and surround me with songs of deliverance. Selah*

2 Thessalonians 3:3 *But the Lord is faithful, and he will strengthen and protect you from the evil one.*

1 Peter 2:24 *"He himself bore our sins" in his body on the cross, so that we might die to sins and live for righteousness; "by his wounds you have been healed."*

Psalm 103:3 *who forgives all your sins and heals all your diseases,*

Psalm 18:2 *The LORD is my rock, my fortress and my Deliverer; my God is my rock, in whom I take refuge. He is my shield and the horn of my salvation, my stronghold.*

Psalm 34:19 *A righteous man may have many troubles, but the LORD delivers him from them all;*

1 Samuel 26:24 *As surely as I valued your life today, so may the LORD value my life and deliver me from all trouble."*

1 Kings 1:29 *The king then took an oath: "As surely as the LORD lives, who has delivered me out of every trouble,*

Now that you see, know and understand that there is a lot of ~ING~ to fully activate the almighty power in the precious blood of the Lamb (Jesus Christ), stop procrastinate~ing~ and start by use~ing~ the ~ING~ factor today.

Start by pray~ing~, speak~ing~, believe~ing~ and receive~ing~ the heal~ing~ over you or someone else. Start by share~ing~ the real and only truth, which are the living words of God to someone. Start by bless~ing~ your life or someone else's life by care~ing and give~ing to the needy and bring~ing~ tithe~ings~ to the church to further the Kingdom of Heaven. Start by provide~ing~ for you family. Start forgive~ing~ anyone for anything as God forgives you. Start by think~ing~ what else you can do to help the needy and further the Kingdom of Heaven. Start by ask~ing~, believe~ing~ and receive~ing~ for everything and anything according to the riches and glory in Christ Jesus. Start by seek~ing~ to find. Start by knock~ing~ so it will open. Start by focus~ing~ on God. Remember this;

"Where ever your focus goes, Your energy flows."

Start by hope~ing~ in the Lord. Start by be~ing~ grateful and thankful for everything God has done, will do and will continue to do for you. Start by fear~ing~ the Lord, which is honor~ing~ and reverence~ing~ Him as the King of Kings and Lord of Lords. Start by not grieve~ing~ the Holy Spirit. Start by obey~ing~ God and all of His commandments. Start by acknowledge~ing~ God more. Start by dedicate~ing~ your life to God completely. Start know~ing~ and understand~ing~ God and His live~ing~ words by meditate~ing~ day and night. Start by surrender~ing~ completely and unconditionally to God and His live~ing~ words each and every day. Start by praise~ing~, rejoice~ing~, sing~ing~ and dance~ing~ to the Lord, know~ing~ and understand~ing~ you now can have true joy and true happiness, because of His live~ing~ words. Start by rest~ing~ in the Lord, know~ing~ and understand~ing~ you now have true peace in Him. Start by love~ing~ God know~ing~ and understand~ing~ you now have the true love of God in you. Start by fight~ing~ the good fight of faith.

James 5:13-16 *[13]Is any one of you in trouble? He should pray. Is anyone happy? Let him sing songs of praise.* [14]*Is any one of you sick? He should call the elders of the church to pray over him and anoint him with oil in the name of the Lord.* [15]*And the prayer offered in faith will make the sick person well; the Lord will raise him up. If he has sinned, he will be forgiven.* [16]*Therefore confess your sins to each other and pray for each other so that you may be healed. The prayer of a righteous man is powerful and effective.*

Mark 9:23 *"'If you can'?" said Jesus. "Everything is possible for him who believes."*

Mark 11:22-24 *"Have faith in God," Jesus answered.* [23]*"I tell you the truth, if anyone says to this mountain, 'Go, throw yourself into the sea,' and does not doubt in his heart but believes that what he says will happen, it will be done for him.* [24]*Therefore I tell you, whatever you ask for in prayer, believe that you have received it, and it will be yours.*

Malachi 3:10 *Bring the whole tithe into the storehouse, that there may be food in my house. Test me in this," says the LORD Almighty, "and see if I will not throw open the floodgates of heaven and pour out so much blessing that you will not have room enough for it.*

Ephesians 4:30 *And do not grieve the Holy Spirit of God, with whom you were sealed for the day of redemption.*

Matthew 7:7 [*Ask, Seek, Knock*] *"Ask and it will be given to you; seek and you will find; knock and the door will be opened to you.*

Matthew 7:8 *For everyone who asks receives; the one who seeks finds; and to the one who knocks, the door will be opened.*

Matthew 11:28-30 ^{28} *"Come to me, all you who are weary and burdened, and I will give you rest. ^{29} Take my yoke upon you and learn from me, for I am gentle and humble in heart, and you will find rest for your souls. ^{30} For my yoke is easy and my burden is light."*

Psalm 62:1 *Truly my soul finds rest in God; my salvation comes from him.*

Jeremiah 17:7 *"But blessed is the one who trusts in the LORD, whose confidence is in him.*

Jeremiah 29:11 *For I know the plans I have for you,"* declares the LORD, *"plans to prosper you and not to harm you, plans to give you hope and a future.*

Romans 15:13 declares that, *May the God of hope fill you with all joy and peace as you trust in him, so that you may overflow with hope by the power of the Holy Spirit.*

Psalm 33:8 *Let all the earth fear the LORD; let all the people of the world revere him.*

Psalm 86:11 *Teach me your way, O LORD, and I will walk in your truth; give me an undivided heart, that I may fear your name.*

Proverbs 1:7 *The fear of the LORD is the beginning of knowledge, but fools despise wisdom and discipline.*

Philippians 4:4 *Rejoice in the Lord always. I will say it again: Rejoice!*

1 Chronicles 16:34 *Give thanks to the LORD, for he is good; his love endures forever.*

Ephesians 5:20 *always giving thanks to God the Father for everything, in the name of our Lord Jesus Christ.*

1Thessalonians 5:18 *Give thanks in all circumstances, for this is God's will for you in Christ Jesus.*

Mark 11: 25 *And when you stand praying, if you hold anything against anyone, forgive him, so that your Father in heaven may forgive you your sins. "*

1 Timothy 6:12 *Fight the good fight of the faith. Take hold of the eternal life to which you were called when you made your good confession in the presence of many witnesses.*

2 Timothy 4:7 *I have fought the good fight, I have finished the race, I have kept the faith.*

So now you can truly see how much ~ING~ factor you can use to activate the power, protection and authority in the precious blood of the Lamb Jesus Christ.

Matthew 16:19 *I will give you the keys of the kingdom of heaven; whatever you bind on earth will be bound in heaven, and whatever you loose on earth will be loosed in heaven."*

Deuteronomy 30:19 *This day I call heaven and earth as witnesses against you that I have set before you life and death, blessings and curses. Now choose life, so that you and your children may live.*

Proverbs 18:21 *The tongue has the power of life and death and those who love it will eat its fruit.*

Also you must be very careful not to use the ~ING~ factor in a negative way, because words are very powerful and Satan knows it. He is smarter than you think. Remember he was an angel of the Lord before He became a fallen angel. He is all about getting you to begin by fear~ing~ death, so that you will become weaken in not believe~ing_in the Lord's live~ing~ words, so he can then try Kill~ing~, robb~ing~, distroy~ing~, murder~ing~ and devour~ing~ you and everything God has create, but he has no power to defeat God. Remember he is skilled at lie~ing~ and convincing God's people to listen to his lies. Jesus tells us that there is no truth in the devil, and even goes so far as to say that lying is the devil's native language and that he is the father of lies.

John 8:44 *You belong to your father, the devil, and you want to carry out your father's desire. He was a murderer from the beginning, not holding to the truth, for there is no truth in him. When he lies, he speaks his native language, for he is a liar and the father of lies.*

Revelation 21 (Amplified Bible) *But as for the cowards and the ignoble and the contemptible and the cravenly lacking in courage and the cowardly submissive, and as for the unbelieving and faithless, and as for the depraved and defiled with abominations, and as for murderers and the lewd and adulterous and the practicers of magic arts and the idolaters (those who give supreme devotion to anyone or anything other than God) and all liars (those who knowingly convey untruth by word or deed)--[all of these shall have] their part in the lake that blazes with fire and brimstone. This is the second death.*

Well, the good news is that, you have the power, protection and authority given in you by God through His Holy Spirit, so that you can start by instruct~ing~, bind~ing~ and command~ing~ Satan and his many demons to flee from you and your family if they try to harm you or your family. That's why it so very important to learn to know and understand the live~ing~ words of God and His power, protection and authority He has given you through His Holy Spirit, so you can live your life in complete victory over Satan and his demons.

So now you see that you can use a lot of the ~ING~ factor to fully activate God's Almighty Power in the precious blood of the Lamb Jesus Christ and our Redeemer who is risen and lives inside His people. Praise the Lord! Our Redeemer lives! The victory is ours in Christ Jesus! Amen.

Chapter 6

Conquering the Spirit of Fear with God's Almighty Power, Protection & Authority That Is in the Precious Blood of the Lamb Jesus Christ

2 Timothy 1:7(KJV) *For God hath not given us the spirit of fear; but of power, and of love, and of a sound mind.*

As you see in the above Bible scripture that fear is a spirit not of God, but of Satan. God did not give us a spirit of fear, but what He did give us is His power, protection and authority to use that will conquer all. He also gave us a sound mind, which we have the ability to be in control of, if we choose to do so.

So with that said, the only thing you need to fear is God, which is to acknowledge Him by loving Him with all your heart, mind and soul by honoring and giving reverence to Him constantly as your Master and the Lord of your salvation.

Mark 12:30 *Love the Lord your God with all your heart and with all your soul and with all your mind and with all your strength. '*

When you do this all your focus will be totally on God and you will not have time to pay attention to Satan and his evil lies and tricks always trying to get your focus off God and His living words.

James 4:7 *Submit yourselves, then, to God. Resist the devil, and he will flee from you.*

The only weapon that Satan and his demons have to try and harm you is the spirit of fear. You see Satan know his time is short on this earth, because Jesus has already conquered the spirit of fear (death) through His resurrection.

The spirit of fear is equals to death, but Jesus through His resurrection is equal to life. To prove that when Satan causes you to fear something you really fear death, I am going to give you some examples;

Let just say, you tell me you have a fear of heights. Well, you don't. It's not the height you are in fear of, it's the possibility of you falling and hitting the ground and dying that you really fear, which is death.

Ok how about another example. Let's say you tell me you have a fear of snakes. Well, again you don't fear snakes, you fear getting bit from it and dying, which again the fear equals death.

Any fear you have, the end result from that fear is that you fear death and Satan knows it. That is why Satan and his demons will do everything and anything in their power to get you to completely focus off God and His living words, so you might become weak in your trust and faith in believing in God and His living words that he will try to devour you like a roaring lion.

Well there is Good News, you have the power, protection and authority of almighty God that's inside you to conquer this spirit of fear through the precious blood of the Lamb (Jesus Christ) and Satan knows it. You were redeemed at the cross at Calvary, where you were purchased for a price and your salvation is in the Lord, which equals eternal life, not death. You cannot die.

Psalm 118:17 *I will not die but live, and will proclaim what the LORD has done.*

When Jesus said you will not perish and have everlasting life, He means it. The curse of death, hell and the grave is already won, but you need to trust and have the faith to believe God and His living words. You cannot die. Jesus said, you would not perish, meaning you cannot die, so why would you fear anything that Satan and his demons will throw at you. Satan is already defeated. The victory is yours already.

John 3:16 (KJV) *[16]For God so loved the world, that he gave his only begotten Son, that whosoever believeth in him should not perish, but have everlasting life.*

When Satan and his demons remind you of your past, remind them of their future. They are finished and already defeated and they have no future, so just laugh at them.

When Satan and his demons remind you of your future, remind them of their past when Jesus broke the curse of death, hell and the grave.

Let Satan and his demons know that you know, you are certified, stamped and covered in the precious blood of the Lamb (Jesus Christ), which is life, not death.

John 5:24 *"Very truly I tell you, whoever hears my word and believes him who sent me has eternal life and will not be judged but has crossed over from death to life.*

Let Satan and his demons also know that you know, you have almighty God's full power, protection and the authority in the blood of the Lamb (Jesus Christ).

Jesus knows how it feels when the spirit of fear tries to take over your mind, heart, soul and body. When Jesus knew that His time of His crucifixion was getting close and He was about to be betrayed by Judas, He got so overwhelmed with sorrow to the point of death that His sweat was like drops of blood falling to the ground.

At this time an angel of the Lord came from Heaven, which strengthened Him. He then got on His knees, the Bible says three time and still asked God our Father to take this cup from Him if it was possible, but each time after praying, Jesus told God may your will be done.

Luke 22:43-44 *[43]An angel from heaven appeared to him and strengthened him. [44] And being in anguish, he prayed more earnestly, and his sweat was like drops of blood falling to the ground.*

What a deep unconditional loving passion and a relentless conviction Jesus had for all of us to break the curse of Satan and by doing the will of the Father when He was tempted by the spirit of fear. Give Him so much praise for what He did at the cross at Calvary. Praise the Lord Almighty for breaking Satan curse of death, hell and the grave. My Redeemer lives and now so can you and I, forever and ever in eternal glory. Praise the Lord!

Matthew 26 36-46 *[36] Then Jesus went with his disciples to a place called Gethsemane, and he said to them, "Sit here while I go over there and pray." [37] He took Peter and the two sons of Zebedee along with him,* *and he began to be sorrowful and troubled. ³⁸ Then he said to them, "My soul is overwhelmed with sorrow to the point of death. Stay here and keep watch with me."*

³⁹ *Going a little farther, he fell with his face to the ground and prayed, "My Father, if it is possible, may this cup be taken from me. Yet not as I will, but as you will."*

⁴⁰ *Then he returned to his disciples and found them sleeping. "Couldn't you men keep watch with me for one hour?" he asked Peter. ⁴¹ "Watch and pray so that you will not fall into temptation. The spirit is willing, but the flesh is weak."*

⁴² *He went away a second time and prayed, "My Father, if it is not possible for this cup to be taken away unless I drink it, may your will be done."*

⁴³ *When he came back, he again found them sleeping, because their eyes were heavy. ⁴⁴ So he left them and went away once more and prayed the third time, saying the same thing.*

⁴⁵ *Then he returned to the disciples and said to them, "Are you still sleeping and resting? Look, the hour has come, and the Son of Man is delivered into the hands of sinners. ⁴⁶ Rise! Let us go! Here comes my betrayer!"*

Since Satan and his demons only weapon they have is the spirits of fear, don't give into it. That's the only thing they have to try to control you or paralyze you with.

There time is short, so fight the good fight of faith by knowing and understanding the living words of God.

1 Timothy 6:12 *Fight the good fight of the faith. Take hold of the eternal life to which you were called when you made your good confession in the presence of many witnesses.*

Remember you have Almighty God's awesome power, protection and His authority that lives in you through His Holy Spirit, which certifies, stamps, seals and covers you by the precious blood of the Lamb Jesus Christ that conquered and broke the curse of Satan (death) and cleansed us from all sins, so we would not perish and live life eternally in Heaven with God the Father.

Ephesians 4:30 *And do not grieve the Holy Spirit of God, with whom you were sealed for the day of redemption.*

Romans 4:7 *"Blessed are those whose transgressions are forgiven, whose sins are covered.*

So now you that know how and why you can conquer the spirit of fear, here are 4 steps to help you do it:

Steps 1: (Admit) all your fears without shame, because we all can feel it even like Jesus felt it prior to His crucifixion, when he got on His knees and prayed three times to God the Father to take this cup from Him if it was possible.

Step 2: (Submit) all your fears to God through prayer and by totally surrendering to Him and His living words, so you can begin to trust in God and have the faith to believe what has done and will do for us that is recorded in the Bible.

That's why it is so important to get to know God on a personal level by having a personal relationship with Him, so that you will know without a doubt that you can put all your trust in Him with all your heart, mind and soul and have the faith to believe He can and will do all that He promises that are recorded in the Bible.

How can you trust in someone you don't really know anyways? You can't, so I recommend that you get to really know Him more by meditating each day and night on Him and His living words and communicating to him by praying more on a regular basic.

"If you want to starve a monster, Don't Feed It!"

Step 3: (Focus) on the presence of God and His unconditional love towards us, which will bring you in the fullness of His joy. How can you fear anything in the presence of the Lord? You can't, because in the presence of God there is life not death, light not darkness, true joy not sadness, true love not hate, true peace not Turmoil, true happiness not depression, gloom, misery, pain, sadness or sorrow. Get the point. Keep your focus on the Lord always.

STEP 4: (Face) your fears with faith. Fight the good fight of faith. God has all ready conquered the spirit of fear through His resurrection. The battle is already won and victory is already yours, so resist Satan and his demons and they will flee for you. Satan and his many demons already know that you have God's almighty power, protection and authority that lives inside you through His Holy Spirit, which you are covered, stamped and sealed by the precious blood of the Lamb Jesus Christ that has already conquered the spirit of fear through His resurrection and now you know it. So give the Lord Praise and Worship, because we will always have the Victory over Satan.

Mark 12:30 *Love the Lord your God with all your heart and with all your soul and with all your mind and with all your strength.'*

John 16:33 *"I have told you these things, so that in me you may have peace. In this world you will have trouble. But take heart! I have overcome the world."*

1 Timothy 6:12 *Fight the good fight of the faith. Take hold of the eternal life to which you were called when you made your good confession in the presence of many witnesses.*

2 Timothy 1:7(KJV) *For God hath not given us the spirit of fear; but of power, and of love, and of a sound mind.*

1 John 4:4 (KJV) *Greater is he that is in you, than he that is in the world.*

Philippians 4:13 (KJV) *I can do all things through Christ which strengtheneth me.*

Romans 8:31 *If God is for us, who can be against us?*

1 Samuel 12:16 *"Now then, stand still and see this great thing the LORD is about to do before your eyes!*

Isaiah 41:10 (Amplified Bible) *Fear not [there is nothing to fear], for I am with you; do not look around you in terror and be dismayed, for I am your God. I will strengthen and harden you to difficulties, yes, I will help you; yes, I will hold you up and retain you with My [victorious] right hand of rightness and justice.*

James 4:7 *Submit yourselves, then, to God. Resist the devil, and he will flee from you.*

Chapter 7

Conquering the Spirit of Unforgiveness with God's Almighty Power, Protection & Authority That Is in the Precious Blood of the Lamb Jesus Christ

Mark 11: 25 *And when you stand praying, if you hold anything against anyone, forgive him, so that your Father in heaven may forgive you your sins."*

This chapter is one of the most important chapters you will ever read and you want to pay very close attention to it, because if you don't understand and do what the words of God say to do about forgiveness, it will stop you from entering the Kingdom of Heaven.

I fully know that this is a very powerful statement to make about God's living words and I know many will try to contest it, but if you believe the living words of God in the Bible, I hope God's words will speak to your heart, mind and soul the real and only truth, which I will be sharing with you.

I love each and every one of you unconditionally and want to see us all in Heaven for eternity and not go to hell, because of lack of knowledge or assuming that you think you know what the words of God mean, instead of truly knowing it and obeying it.

Joshua 1:8 *Do not let this Book of the Law depart from your mouth; meditate on it day and night, so that you may be careful to do everything written in it. Then you will be prosperous and successful.*

The above Bible scripture is such a key verse that will help us all to know, understand and do what the entire living words of God say for us to do, so that we know what it really takes on our behalf to enter the Kingdom of Heaven.

Many Christian people still don't fully understand the true power of God's forgiveness and what it did for us, what it can do for us and what it will do to us if we choose not to forgive.

Matthew 6:14 *For if you forgive other people when they sin against you, your heavenly Father will also forgive you.*

Matthew 6:15 *But if you do not forgive others their sins, your Father will not forgive your sins.*

It was Jesus that first demonstrated the almighty power of forgiveness on the cross at Calvary, when He redeemed us by shedding His precious blood for all of our sins and breaking Satan's curse of death, hell and the grave, so we could have eternal life.

John 3:16 (KJV) *[16]For God so loved the world, that he gave his only begotten Son, that whosoever believeth in him should not perish, but have everlasting life.*

1 Peter 2:24 *"He himself bore our sins" in his body on the cross, so that we might die to sins and live for righteousness; "by his wounds you have been healed."*

Hebrews 9:22 *In fact, the law requires that nearly everything be cleansed with blood, and without the shedding of blood there is no forgiveness.*

Ephesians 1:7 *In him we have redemption through his blood, the forgiveness of sins, in accordance with the riches of God's grace.*

Romans 10:9 (KJV) *That if thou shalt confess with thy mouth the Lord Jesus, and shalt believe in thine heart that God hath raised him from the dead, thou shalt be saved.*

John 1:9 *If we confess our sins, he is faithful and just and will forgive us our sins and purify us from all unrighteousness.*

Matthew 26:28 *This is my blood of the covenant, which is poured out for many for the forgiveness of sins.*

Hebrews 8:12 *For I will forgive their wickedness and will remember their sins no more."*

Psalm 130:4 *But with you there is forgiveness, so that we can, with reverence, serve you.*

Jeremiah 33:8 *I will cleanse them from all the sin they have committed against me and will forgive all their sins of rebellion against me.*

James 5:15 *And the prayer offered in faith will make the sick person well; the Lord will raise them up. If they have sinned, they will be forgiven.*

Galatians 3:13 *Christ redeemed us from the curse of the law by becoming a curse for us, for it is written: "Cursed is everyone who is hung on a pole."*

Revelation 22:3 *No longer will there be any curse. The throne of God and of the Lamb will be in the city, and his servants will serve him.*

Jesus forgave us all unconditionally and asked our Father to forgive us all, even when we didn't know what we were doing. He did this one, because He wants us all to have the chance to make it into Heaven and two, because He knows that any unclean spirits cannot be in the presence of God the Father in Heaven.

Luke 23:34 *Jesus said, "Father, forgive them, for they do not know what they are doing."*

We must be pure in heart and our sins must not just be covered, but cleansed whiter than snow by the shedding of the precious blood of the Lamb Jesus Christ when He went to the cross for us at Calvary.

Titus 2:11-14 *For the grace of God that brings salvation has appeared to all men. It teaches us to say "No" to ungodliness and worldly passions, and to live self-controlled, upright and godly lives in this present age, while we wait for the blessed hope—the glorious appearing of our great God and Savior, Jesus Christ, who gave himself for us to redeem us from all wickedness and to purify for himself a people that are his very own, eager to do what is good.*

God the Father is Pure and Holy and will not tolerate any impure hearts or sins in Heaven in His presence. Do you think for a moment that there are people in Heaven right now that are still holding grudges towards someone, because of unforgiveness they had towards that person? I hope you said no, because unforgiveness is a sin, that you and only you have the almighty power to conquer it through the Holy Spirit that lives inside you, because of Jesus redeeming us by shedding His precious blood on the cross at Calvary for all of our sins.

1 Peter 1:13-16 *Therefore, prepare your minds for action; be self-controlled; set your hope fully on the grace to be given you when Jesus Christ is revealed. As obedient children, do not conform to the evil desires you had when you lived in ignorance. But just as he who called you is holy, so be holy in all you do; for it is written: "Be holy, because I am holy."*

That's why Jesus' livings words in the Bible say many times, that we should forgive other people when they sin against us, so our Heavenly Father will also forgive us. If we don't our Father in Heaven will not forgive us and we will not enter the Kingdom of Heaven with the sin of unforgiveness.

How can you honestly ask and want God to forgive you for everything and anything you have done, but not forgive others for the same things? You can't, not just because morally it's seem wrong, but because the living words of God say so. Here are some Bible scripture pertaining to that;

Matthew 6:12 *And forgive us our debts, as we also have forgiven our debtors.*

Matthew 6:14 *For if you forgive other people when they sin against you, your heavenly Father will also forgive you.*

Matthew 6:15 *But if you do not forgive others their sins, your Father will not forgive your sins.*

Matthew 9:5 *Which is easier: to say, 'Your sins are forgiven,' or to say, 'Get up and walk'?*

Matthew 9:6 *But I want you to know that the Son of Man has authority on earth to forgive sins." So he said to the paralyzed man, "Get up, take your mat and go home."*

Matthew 18:21 *Then Peter came to Jesus and asked, "Lord, how many times shall I forgive my brother or sister who sins against me? Up to seven times?"*

Matthew 18:35 *"This is how my heavenly Father will treat each of you unless you forgive your brother or sister from your heart."*

Luke 17:3 *So watch yourselves. "If your brother or sister sins against you, rebuke them; and if they repent, forgive them.*

Luke 17:4 *Even if they sin against you seven times in a day and seven times come back to you saying 'I repent,' you must forgive them."*

John 20:23 *If you forgive anyone's sins, their sins are forgiven; if you do not forgive them, they are not forgiven."*

2 Corinthians 2:7 *Now instead, you ought to forgive and comfort him, so that he will not be overwhelmed by excessive sorrow.*

2 Corinthians 2:10 *Anyone you forgive, I also forgive. And what I have forgiven—if there was anything to forgive—I have forgiven in the sight of Christ for your sake,*

Colossians 3:13 *Bear with each other and forgive one another if any of you has a grievance against someone. Forgive as the Lord forgave you.*

As you see in the above Bible scriptures that Jesus is crystal clear about forgiving others, so that our Father in Heaven will forgive us. God is the only true man of His words and you can trust Him at His words. He will not go against what His living words say or He would not be Holy and Righteous. If God said you will not be forgiven if you do not forgive, then you can rest assure that you will not enter the Kingdom of Heaven with the Sin of unforgiveness.

Hebrews 10:23 *Let us hold fast the profession of our faith without wavering; (for he is faithful that promised;)*

God is the same yesterday, today and forever His words never changes, not like how the world tries to change it, so it would fit into their life style. I trust God's words period, not what the world says is ok. Remember Satan and His demons are of the world and will do everything and anything to confuse you and try to distort the real and only truth, which is the living words of God. Don't be fooled by the father of lies (Satan and his demons).

Hebrews 13:8 *Jesus Christ is the same yesterday and today and forever.*

Also the living words of God in the Bible are crystal clear about not judging others. So do not judge others and you will not be judged. Do not condemn others and you will not be condemned. For whoever judges other will be judge according to how they judge others.

God is no respecter of person and He loves everyone the same. So who gives us the authority to judge someone else? The answer is, no one did. Even Jesus said, "I did not come to judge the world, but to save the world." Are we better then Him? I think not, as a matter a fact, I know that I'm not and hope you do to. God the Father is the Judge and the only judge and even judges the highest.

Job 21:22 *Can anyone teach knowledge to God, since he judges even the highest?*

Luke 6:37 *"Do not judge, and you will not be judged. Do not condemn, and you will not be condemned. Forgive, and you will be forgiven.*

John 12:47 *"If anyone hears my words but does not keep them, I do not judge that person. For I did not come to judge the world, but to save the world.*

John 12:48 *There is a judge for the one who rejects me and does not accept my words; the very words I have spoken will condemn them at the last day.*

John 8:50 *I am not seeking glory for myself; but there is one who seeks it, and he is the judge.*

2 Timothy 4:8 *Now there is in store for me the crown of righteousness, which the Lord, the righteous Judge, will award to me on that day—and not only to me, but also to all who have longed for his appearing.*

1 Corinthians 4:4 *My conscience is clear, but that does not make me innocent. It is the Lord who judges me*

1 Corinthians 11:32 *Nevertheless, when we are judged in this way by the Lord, we are being disciplined so that we will not be finally condemned with the world.*

1 Corinthians 4:5 *Therefore judge nothing before the appointed time; wait until the Lord comes. He will bring to light what is hidden in darkness and will expose the*

motives of the heart. At that time each will receive their praise from God.

2 Corinthians 10:7 *You are judging by appearances. If anyone is confident that they belong to Christ, they should consider again that we belong to Christ just as much as they do.*

James 4:11 *Brothers and sisters, do not slander one another. Anyone who speaks against a brother or sister or judges them speaks against the law and judges it. When you judge the law, you are not keeping it, but sitting in judgment on it.*

Also I try to be very careful what I say to someone about the living words of God, because I know I will be held to a higher standard and be judged more strictly in God's eyes. There are many people that teach the gospel of Jesus Christ and do a great job, but as you know there are and will be some coming that many people will be fooled by them and the living words in the Bible warns us about them. They will come in sheep's clothing, but inwardly they are ferocious wolves. Also the living words of God declare that we will recognize them by their fruit.

James 3:1 *Not many of you should become teachers, my fellow believers, because you know that we who teach will be judged more strictly.*

Matthew 7:15-16 [15]*"Watch out for false prophets. They come to you in sheep's clothing, but inwardly they are ferocious wolves. [16]By their fruit you will recognize them. Do people pick grapes from thorn bushes, or figs from thistles?*

There is also one more thing about forgiveness that you should know. God will forgive us all for everything and anything we do, except for blasphemy against the Holy Spirit, which you will not be forgiven for.

Matthew 12:31 *And so I tell you, every kind of sin and slander can be forgiven, but blasphemy against the Spirit will not be forgiven.*

Matthew 12:32 *Anyone who speaks a word against the Son of Man will be forgiven, but anyone who speaks against the Holy Spirit will not be forgiven, either in this age or in the age to come.*

Many people still think there are many ways they can get to Heaven, but if you follow and believe the real and only truth (the living words of God), there is only one way and that way is through Jesus Christ.

John 14:6 *Jesus answered, "I am the way and the truth and the life. No one comes to the Father except through me.*

Also many people will think they are going to Heaven because of their good works here on earth, which they done in the name of the Lord, but not all will make it. The living words of God declare that Jesus will say to them. "Depart from me." It could be as simple as unforgiveness, a grudge you have towards someone and never completely forgave them. Sin is sin and God will not tolerate any kind of it in His presence in Heaven.

Matthew 25:41 *"Then he will say to those on his left, 'Depart from me, you who are cursed, into the eternal fire prepared for the devil and his angels.*

Habakkuk 1:13 *Your eyes are too pure to look on evil; you cannot tolerate wrongdoing.*

The best way to conquer unforgiveness is to get the true God love inside you by making a choice, a decision to allow Jesus to come and live in your heart as your Lord and Savior. Once you surrender unconditionally to Him and His living words and open His divine gift that's inside you, you will begin to know and understand what true unconditional God love is and you will eventually become more of that God love inside you to be able to forgive anyone for anything just like Jesus did. You will then not be able to tolerate sin or unforgiveness in your heart anymore, because of the God love. Here is one of the greatest Bible scriptures on true unconditional God love;

1 Corinthians 13 1-13 *¹If I speak in the tongues of men and of angels, but have not love, I am only a resounding gong or a clanging cymbal. ²If I have the gift of prophecy*

and can fathom all mysteries and all knowledge, and if I have a faith that can move mountains, but have not love, I am nothing. ³If I give all I possess to the poor and surrender my body to the flames, but have not love, I gain nothing. ⁴Love is patient, love is kind. It does not envy, it does not boast, it is not proud. ⁵It is not rude, it is not self-seeking, it is not easily angered, it keeps no record of wrongs. ⁶Love does not delight in evil but rejoices with the truth. ⁷It always protects, always trusts, always hopes, always perseveres. ⁸Love never fails. But where there are prophecies, they will cease; where there are tongues, they will be stilled; where there is knowledge, it will pass away. ⁹For we know in part and we prophesy in part, ¹⁰but when perfection comes, the imperfect disappears. ¹¹When I was a child, I talked like a child, I thought like a child, I reasoned like a child. When I became a man, I put childish ways behind me. ¹²Now we see but a poor reflection as in a mirror; then we shall see face to face. Now I know in part; then I shall know fully, even as I am fully known. ¹³And now these three remain: faith, hope and love. But the greatest of these is love.

Finally, Jesus tells us how to pray, so that we will know and understand what we need to do to enter the Kingdom of Heaven. In the living words of God in the book of Matthew 6:9-15 Jesus declares,

⁹"This, then, is how you should pray:

Our Father in heaven, hallowed be your name, ¹⁰ your kingdom come, your will be done, on earth as it is in

heaven. [11]Give us today our daily bread. [12]And forgive us our debts, as we also have forgiven our debtors. [13]And lead us not into temptation, but deliver us from the evil one. [14]For if you forgive other people when they sin against you, your heavenly Father will also forgive you. [15]But if you do not forgive others their sins, your Father will not forgive your sins."

Chapter 8

Inspirational Bible Quotes from A To Z

Abundant life

John 10:10 (KJV) *The thief cometh not, but for to steal, and to kill, and to destroy: I am come that they might have life, and that they might have it more abundantly.*

Anger

Leviticus 19:17-18 *Do not hate your brother in your heart. Rebuke your neighbor frankly so you will not share in his guilt. Do not seek revenge or bear a grudge against one of your people, but love your neighbor as yourself. I am the LORD.*

Nehemiah 9:17 *They refused to listen and failed to remember the miracles you performed among them. They became stiff-necked and in their rebellion appointed a leader in order to return to their slavery. But you are a forgiving God, gracious and compassionate, slow to anger and abounding in love. Therefore you did not desert them,*

Psalm 7:11 *God is a righteous judge, a God who expresses his wrath every day.*

Psalm 4:4 *In your anger do not sin; when you are on your beds, search your hearts and be silent.*

Psalm 30:5 *Sing to the LORD, you saints of his; praise his holy name. For his anger lasts only a moment, but his favor lasts a lifetime; weeping may remain for a night, but rejoicing comes in the morning.*

Psalm 37:8 *Refrain from anger and turn from wrath; do not fret—it leads only to evil.*

Psalm 145:8-9 *The LORD is gracious and compassionate, slow to anger and rich in love. The LORD is good to all; he has compassion on all he has made.*

Proverbs 14:17 *A quick-tempered man does foolish things, and a crafty man is hated.*

Proverbs 15:18 *A hot-tempered man stirs up dissension, but a patient man calms a quarrel.*

Proverbs 16:32 *Better a patient man than a warrior, a man who controls his temper than one who takes a city.*

Proverbs 17:14-15 *The beginning of strife is like releasing water; Therefore stop contention before a quarrel starts. He who justifies the wicked, and he who condemns the just, Both of them alike are an abomination to the LORD.*

Proverbs 19:11 *A man's wisdom gives him patience; it is to his glory to overlook an offense.*

Proverbs 20:3 *It is to a man's honor to avoid strife, but every fool is quick to quarrel*

Proverbs 21:19 *Better to live in a desert than with a quarrelsome and ill-tempered wife.*

Proverbs 22:24-25 *Do not make friends with a hot-tempered man, do not associate with one easily angered, or you may learn his ways and get yourself ensnared.*

Proverbs 29:22 *An angry man stirs up dissension, and a hot-tempered one commits many sins.*

Proverbs 30:33 *For as churning the milk produces butter, and as twisting the nose produces blood, so stirring up anger produces strife.*

Ecclesiastes 7:9 *Do not be quickly provoked in your spirit, for anger resides in the lap of fools.*

Matthew 5:22 *But I tell you that anyone who is angry with his brother will be subject to judgment. Again, anyone who says to his brother, 'Raca' is answerable to the Sanhedrin. But anyone who says, 'You fool!' will be in danger of the fire of hell.*

Matthew 21:12-14 *Jesus entered the temple area and drove out all who were buying and selling there. He overturned the tables of the money changers and the benches of those selling doves. 13"It is written," he said to them, " 'My house will be called a house of prayer,'[a] but you are making it a 'den of robbers.'" The blind and the lame came to him at the temple, and he healed them.*

Mark 3:1-2, 5 "He went into the synagogue, and a man with a shriveled hand was there. Some of them were looking for a reason to accuse Jesus, so they watched him closely to see if he would heal him on the Sabbath... He looked around at them in anger and, deeply distressed at their stubborn hearts, said to the man, 'Stretch out your hand.' He stretched it out, and his hand was completely restored."

Romans 12:19-21 *Do not take revenge, my friends, but leave room for God's wrath, for it is written: "It is mine to avenge; I will repay," says the Lord. On the contrary: "If your enemy is hungry, feed him; if he is thirsty, give him something to drink. In doing this, you will heap burning coals on his head." Do not be overcome by evil, but overcome evil with good.*

Colossians 3:7-9 *You used to walk in these ways, in the life you once lived. But now you must rid yourselves of all such things as these: anger, rage, malice, slander, and filthy language from your lips. Do not lie to each other, since you have taken off your old self with its practices*

Colossians 3:21 *Fathers, do not embitter your children, or they will become discouraged.*

Ephesians 4:25-27 *Therefore each of you must put off falsehood and speak truthfully to his neighbor, for we are all members of one body. "In your anger do not sin": Do not let the sun go down while you are still angry, and do not give the devil a foothold.*

Ephesians 4:31-32 *Get rid of all bitterness, rage and anger, brawling and slander, along with every form of malice. Be kind and compassionate to one another, forgiving each other, just as in Christ God forgave you.*

James 1: 17-20 *Every good and perfect gift is from above, coming down from the Father of the heavenly lights, who does not change like shifting shadows. He chose to give us birth through the word of truth that we might be a kind of first fruits of all he created. My dear brothers, take note of this: Everyone should be quick to listen, slow to speak and slow to become angry, for man's anger does not bring about the righteous life that God desires. Therefore, get rid of all moral filth and the evil that is so prevalent and humbly accept the word planted in you, which can save you.*

2 Timothy 2:23-24 *Don't have anything to do with foolish and stupid arguments, because you know they produce quarrels. And the Lord's servant must not quarrel; instead, he must be kind to everyone, able to teach, not resentful*

Anxiety

Philippians 4:6 *Do not be anxious about anything, but in every situation, by prayer and petition, with thanksgiving, present your requests to God.*

Blessings

Genesis 1:22 *God blessed them and said, "Be fruitful and increase in number and fill the water in the seas, and let the birds increase on the earth."*

Genesis 12:2-3 *"I will make you into a great nation and I will bless you; I will make your name great, and you will be a blessing. I will bless those who bless you, and whoever curses you I will curse; and all peoples on earth will be blessed through you."*

Genesis 22:15-18 *The angel of the LORD called to Abraham from heaven a second time and said, "I swear by myself, declares the LORD, that because you have done this and have not withheld your son, your only son, I will surely bless you and make your descendants as numerous as the stars in the sky and as the sand on the seashore. Your descendants will take possession of the cities of their enemies, and through your offspring all nations on earth will be blessed, because you have obeyed me."*

Genesis 26:2-5 *The LORD appeared to Isaac and said, "Do not go down to Egypt; live in the land where I tell you to live. Stay in this land for a while, and I will be with you and will bless you. For to you and your descendants I will give all these lands and will confirm the oath I swore to your father Abraham. I will make your descendants as numerous as the stars in the sky and will give them all these lands, and through your offspring all nations on earth will be blessed, because Abraham obeyed me and kept my requirements, my commands, my decrees and my laws."*

Genesis 48:15-16 *Then he blessed Joseph and said, "May the God before whom my fathers Abraham and Isaac walked, the God who has been my shepherd all my life to this day, the Angel who has delivered me from all harm —may he bless these boys. May they be called by my name and the names of my fathers Abraham and Isaac, and may they increase greatly upon the earth."*

Numbers 6:24-26 *"The LORD bless you and keep you;*

the LORD make his face shine upon you and be gracious to you; the LORD turn his face toward you and give you peace."

Deuteronomy 7:12-15 *If you pay attention to these laws and are careful to follow them, then the LORD your God will keep his covenant of love with you, as he swore to your forefathers. He will love you and bless you and increase your numbers. He will bless the fruit of your womb, the crops of your land—your grain, new wine and oil—the calves of your herds and the lambs of your flocks in the land that he swore to your forefathers to give you. You will be blessed more than any other people; none of your men or women will be childless, nor any of your livestock without young. The LORD will keep you free from every disease.*

Deuteronomy 28:1-12 *If you fully obey the LORD your God and carefully follow all his commands I give you today, the LORD your God will set you high above all the nations on earth. All these blessings will come upon you and accompany you if you obey the LORD your God: You will be blessed in the city and blessed in the country. The fruit of your womb will be blessed, and the crops of your land and the young of your livestock—the calves of your herds and the lambs of your flocks. Your basket and your kneading trough will be blessed. You will be blessed when you come in and blessed when you go out. The LORD will grant that the enemies who rise up against you will be defeated before you. They will come at you from one direction but flee from you in seven. The LORD will send a blessing on your barns and on everything you put your hand to. The LORD your God will bless you in the land he is giving you. The LORD will establish you as his holy people, as he promised you on oath, if you keep the commands of the LORD your God and walk in his ways. Then all the peoples on earth will see that you are called by the name of the LORD, and they will fear you. The LORD will grant you abundant prosperity—in the fruit of your womb, the young of your livestock and the crops of your ground—in the land he swore to your forefathers to give you. The LORD will open the heavens, the storehouse of his bounty, to send rain on your land in season and to bless all the work of your hands. You will lend to many nations but will borrow from none. The LORD will make you the head, not the tail. If you pay attention to the commands of the LORD your God that I give you this day and carefully follow them, you will always be at the top, never at the bottom. 14 Do not turn aside from any of the commands I give you today, to the right or to the left, following other gods and serving them.*

1 Kings 8:56-61 *Praise be to the LORD, who has given rest to his people Israel just as he promised. Not one word has failed of all the good promises he gave through his servant Moses. May the LORD our God be with us as he was with our fathers; may he never leave us nor forsake us. May he turn our hearts to him, to walk in all his ways and to keep the commands, decrees and*

regulations he gave our fathers. And may these words of mine, which I have prayed before the LORD, be near to the LORD our God day and night, that he may uphold the cause of his servant and the cause of his people Israel according to each day's need, so that all the peoples of the earth may know that the LORD is God and that there is no other. But your hearts must be fully committed to the LORD our God, to live by his decrees and obey his commands, as at this time."

Psalm 1:1 *Blessed is the man who does not walk in the counsel of the wicked or stand in the way of sinners or sit in the seat of mockers.*

Psalm 67:1-2 *May God be gracious to us and bless us and make his face shine upon us, that your ways may be known on earth, your salvation among all nations.*

Psalm 121:7-8 *The LORD will keep you from all harm— he will watch over your life; the LORD will watch over your coming and going both now and forevermore.*

Ezekiel 34:25-26 *I will make a covenant of peace with them and rid the land of wild beasts so that they may live in the desert and sleep in the forests in safety. I will bless them and the places surrounding my hill. I will send down showers in season; there will be showers of blessing*

Matthew 5:2-12 *"Blessed are the poor in spirit, for theirs is the kingdom of heaven. Blessed are those who mourn, for they will be comforted. Blessed are the meek, for they will inherit the earth. Blessed are those who hunger and thirst for righteousness, for they will be filled. Blessed are the merciful, for they will be shown mercy. Blessed are the pure in heart, for they will see God. Blessed are the peacemakers, for they will be called sons of God. Blessed are those who are persecuted because of righteousness, for theirs is the kingdom of heaven." Blessed are you when people insult you, persecute you and falsely say all kinds of evil against you because of me. Rejoice and be glad, because great is your reward in heaven, for in the same way they persecuted the prophets who were before you.*

Luke 11:28 *He replied, "Blessed rather are those who hear the word of God and obey it."*

Romans 15:33 *The God of peace be with you all. Amen.*

1 Corinthians 1:3 *Grace and peace to you from God our Father and the Lord Jesus Christ.*

Galatians 6:18 *The grace of our Lord Jesus Christ be with your spirit, sisters and brothers. Amen.*

Ephesians 1:3 *Praise be to the God and Father of our Lord Jesus Christ, who has blessed us in the heavenly realms with every spiritual blessing in Christ.*

Ephesians 3:14-20 *For this reason I kneel before the Father, from whom his whole family in heaven and on earth derives its name. I pray that out of his glorious riches he may strengthen you with power through his Spirit in your inner being, so that Christ may dwell in your hearts through faith. And I pray that you, being rooted and established in love, 1may have power, together with all the believers, to grasp how wide and long and high and deep is the love of Christ, and to know this love that surpasses knowledge--that you may be filled to the measure of all the fullness of God. Now to him who is able to do immeasurably more than all we ask or imagine, according to his power that is at work within us, to him be glory in the church and in Christ Jesus throughout all generations, for ever and ever! Amen.*

Colossians 1:9-12 *For this reason, since the day we heard about you, we have not stopped praying for you and asking God to fill you with the knowledge of his will through all spiritual wisdom and understanding. And we pray this in order that you may live a life worthy of the Lord and may please him in every way: bearing fruit in every good work, growing in the knowledge of God, being strengthened with all power according to his glorious might so that you may have great endurance and patience, and joyfully giving thanks to the Father, who has qualified you to share in the inheritance.... in the kingdom of light.*

James 1:12 *Blessed is the man who perseveres under trial, because when he has stood the test, he will receive*

the crown of life that God has promised to those who love
him.

3 John 2 (KJV) *"Beloved, I wish above all things that
thou mayest prosper and be in health, even as thy soul
prospereth."*

Revelation 1:3 *Blessed is the one who reads the words
of this prophecy, and blessed are those who hear it and
take to heart what is written in it, because the time is
near.*

Citizenship

Romans 13:1-7 *Everyone must submit himself to the
governing authorities, for there is no authority except
that which God has established. The authorities that exist
have been established by God. Consequently, he who
rebels against the authority is rebelling against what
God has instituted, and those who do so will bring
judgment on themselves. For rulers hold no terror for
those who do right, but for those who do wrong. Do you
want to be free from fear of the one in authority? Then do
what is right and he will commend you. For he is God's
servant to do you good. But if you do wrong, be afraid,
for he does not bear the sword for nothing. He is God's
servant, an agent of wrath to bring punishment on the
wrongdoer. Therefore, it is necessary to submit to the
authorities, not only because of possible punishment but
also because of conscience. This is also why you pay*

taxes, for the authorities are God's servants, who give their full time to governing. Give everyone what you owe him: If you owe taxes, pay taxes; if revenue, then revenue; if respect, then respect; if honor, then honor.

Titus 3:1 *Remind the people to be subject to rulers and authorities, to be obedient, to be ready to do whatever is good.*

Cleanliness

2 Corinthians 7:1 *Since we have these promises, dear friends, let us purify ourselves from everything that contaminates body and spirit, perfecting holiness out of reverence for God.*

Consecration

Romans 12:1,2 *Therefore, I urge you, brothers, in view of God's mercy, to offer your bodies as living sacrifices, holy and pleasing to God—this is your spiritual act of worship. Do not conform any longer to the pattern of this world, but be transformed by the renewing of your mind. Then you will be able to test and approve what God's will is—his good, pleasing and perfect will.*

Contentment

Philippians 4:11-13 *I am not saying this because I am in need, for I have learned to be content whatever the* circumstances. *I know what it is to be in need, and I know what it is to have plenty. I have learned the secret of being content in any and every situation, whether well fed or hungry, whether living in plenty or in want. I can do everything through him who gives me strength.*

1 Timothy 6:6 *But godliness with contentment is great gain.*

Courage

Psalm 27:14 *Wait for the LORD; be strong and take heart and wait for the LORD.*

1 John 4:4 (KJV) *Greater is he that is in you, than he that is in the world.*

Philippians 4:13 (KJV) *I can do all things through Christ which strengtheneth me.*

Romans 8:31 *If God is for us, who can be against us?*

1 Samuel 12:16 *"Now then, stand still and see this great thing the LORD is about to do before your eyes!*

Isaiah 41:10 (Amplified Bible) *Fear not [there is nothing to fear], for I am with you; do not look around you in terror and be dismayed, for I am your God. I will strengthen and harden you to difficulties, yes, I will help you; yes, I will hold you up and retain you with My [victorious] right hand of rightness and justice.*

Psalm 18:2 *The LORD is my rock, my fortress and my deliverer; my God is my rock, in whom I take refuge. He is my shield and the horn of my salvation, my stronghold.*

2 Timothy 1 (KJV) *For God hath not given us the spirit of fear; but of power, and of love, and of a sound mind.*

Deliverance

Psalm 34:19 *A righteous man may have many troubles, but the LORD delivers him from them all;*

1 Samuel 26:24 *As surely as I valued your life today, so may the LORD value my life and deliver me from all trouble."*

1 Kings 1:29 *The king then took an oath: "As surely as the LORD lives, who has delivered me out of every trouble,*

2 Kings 17:39 *Rather, worship the LORD your God; it is he who will deliver you from the hand of all your enemies."*

Psalm 6:4 *Turn, O LORD, and deliver me; save me because of your unfailing love.*

Job 36:15 (KJV) *He delivereth the poor in his affliction, and openeth their ears in oppression.*

2 Peter 2; 9 (KJV) *The Lord knoweth how to deliver the godly out of temptations, and to reserve the unjust unto the day of judgment to be punished:*

Psalm 34:4 *I sought the LORD, and he answered me; he delivered me from all my fears.*

Hebrews 2:14-15 (KJV) *[14]Forasmuch then as the children are partakers of flesh and blood, he also himself likewise took part of the same; that through death he might destroy him that had the power of death, that is, the devil; [15]And deliver them who through fear of death were all their lifetime subject to bondage.*

2 Timothy 4:17 (KJV) *Notwithstanding the Lord stood with me, and strengthened me; that by me the preaching might be fully known, and that all the Gentiles might hear: and I was delivered out of the mouth of the lion.*

Matthew 6:13 (KJV) *And lead us not into temptation, but deliver us from evil: For thine is the kingdom, and the power, and the glory, for ever. Amen.*

2 Corinthians 1:8-10 *[8]For we would not, brethren, have you ignorant of our trouble which came to us in Asia, that we were pressed out of measure, above strength, insomuch that we despaired even of life: [9]But we had the sentence of death in ourselves, that we should not trust in ourselves, but in God which raiseth the dead:*

[10]*Who delivered us from so great a death, and doth deliver: in whom we trust that he will yet deliver us;*

Diligence

Romans 12:11 *Never be lacking in zeal, but keep your spiritual fervor, serving the Lord.*

Duty

Luke 20:21-25 *So the spies questioned him: "Teacher, we know that you speak and teach what is right, and that you do not show partiality but teach the way of God in accordance with the truth. Is it right for us to pay taxes to Caesar or not?" He saw through their duplicity and said to them, "Show me a denarius. Whose portrait and inscription are on it?" "Caesar's," they replied. He said to them, "Then give to Caesar what is Caesar's, and to God what is God's."*

Endurance

Luke 21:9-19 *When you hear of wars and revolutions, do not be frightened. These things must happen first, but the end will not come right away. "Then he said to them: "Nation will rise against nation, and kingdom against kingdom. There will be great earthquakes, famines and pestilences in various places, and fearful events and great signs from heaven. "But before all this, they will lay hands on you and persecute you. They will deliver you to synagogues and prisons, and you will be brought before kings and governors, and all on account of my name. This will result in your being witnesses to them. But make up your mind not to worry beforehand how you will defend yourselves. For I will give you words and wisdom that none of your adversaries will be able to resist or contradict. You will be betrayed even by parents, brothers, relatives and friends, and they will put some of you to death. All men will hate you because of me. But not a hair of your head will perish. By standing firm you will gain life.*

2 Timothy 2:3 *Endure hardship with us like a good soldier of Christ Jesus.*

Faith

Hebrews 11:1 (KJV) *Now faith is the substance of things hoped for, the evidence of things not seen.*

Matthew 8:5-13 *When Jesus had entered Capernaum, a centurion came to him, asking for help. "Lord," he said, "my servant lies at home paralyzed and in terrible suffering." Jesus said to him, "I will go and heal him." The centurion replied, "Lord, I do not deserve to have you come under my roof. But just say the word, and my servant will be healed. For I myself am a man under authority, with soldiers under me. I tell this one, 'Go,' and he goes; and that one, 'Come,' and he comes. I say to my servant, 'Do this,' and he does it." When Jesus heard this, he was astonished and said to those following him, "I tell you the truth, I have not found anyone in Israel with such great faith. I say to you that many will come from the east and the west, and will take their places at the feast with Abraham, Isaac and Jacob in the kingdom of heaven. But the subjects of the kingdom will be thrown outside, into the darkness, where there will be weeping and gnashing of teeth." Then Jesus said to the centurion, "Go! It will be done just as you believed it would." And his servant was healed at that very hour.*

Mark 11:22-24 *"Have faith in God," Jesus answered. "I tell you the truth, if anyone says to this mountain, 'Go, throw yourself into the sea,' and does not doubt in his heart but believes that what he says will happen, it will be done for him. Therefore I tell you, whatever you ask for in prayer, believe that you have received it, and it will be yours.*

1 Timothy 6:12 *Fight the good fight of the faith. Take hold of the eternal life to which you were called when you made your good confession in the presence of many witnesses.*

Romans 10:17 (KJV) *"So then faith cometh by hearing, and hearing by the word of God."*

Hebrews 11:1(KJV) *Now faith is the substance of things hoped for, the evidence of things not seen*

Hebrews 11:6 *And without faith it is impossible to please God, because anyone who comes to him must believe that he exists and that he rewards those who earnestly seek him.*

Mark 9:23 *"'If you can'?" said Jesus. "Everything is possible for him who believes."*

Faithfulness

Matthew 25:23 *His master replied, 'Well done, good and faithful servant! You have been faithful with a few things; I will put you in charge of many things. Come and share your master's happiness!'*

Hebrews 10:23 *Let us hold fast the profession of our faith without wavering; (for he is faithful that promised;)*

John 15:7 *If you remain in me and my words remain in you, ask whatever you wish, and it will be given you.*

1 Timothy 4:1 *The Spirit clearly says that in later times some will abandon the faith and follow deceiving spirits and things taught by demons.*

Joshua 24:15 *But if serving the LORD seems undesirable to you, then choose for yourselves this day whom you will serve, whether the gods your forefathers served beyond the River, or the gods of the Amorites, in whose land you are living. But as for me and my household, we will serve the LORD."*

2 Timothy 4:7 *I have fought the good fight, I have finished the race, I have kept the faith.*

Job 19:25 *I know that my Redeemer lives, and that in the end he will stand upon the earth.*

Forgiveness

Mark 11:25-26 *And when you stand praying, if you hold anything against anyone, forgive him, so that your Father in heaven may forgive you your sins."*

Ephesians 4:31-32 *Get rid of all bitterness, rage and anger, brawling and slander, along with every form of malice. Be kind and compassionate to one another, forgiving each other, just as in Christ God forgave you.*

Luke 6:27 *"But to you who are listening I say: Love your enemies, do good to those who hate you,"*

Freedom

John 8:31-36 *To the. Jews who had believed him, Jesus said, "If you hold to my teaching, you are really my disciples. Then you will know the truth, and the truth will set you free."They answered him, "We are Abraham's descendants[a] and have never been slaves of anyone. How can you say that we shall be set free? "Jesus replied, "I tell you the truth, everyone who sins is a slave to sin. Now a slave has no permanent place in the family, but a son belongs to it forever. So if the Son sets you free, you will be free indeed.*

Fruitfulness

John 15:1-8 *"I am the true vine, and my Father is the gardener. He cuts off every branch in me that bears no fruit, while every branch that does bear fruit he prunes so that it will be even more fruitful. You are already clean because of the word I have spoken to you. Remain in me, and I will remain in you. No branch can bear fruit by itself; it must remain in the vine. Neither can you bear fruit unless you remain in me. "I am the vine; you are the branches. If a man remains in me and I in him, he will bear much fruit; apart from me you can do nothing. If anyone does not remain in me, he is like a branch that is thrown away and withers; such branches are picked up, thrown into the fire and burned. If you remain in me and my words remain in you, ask whatever you wish, and it will be given you. This is to my Father's glory, that you bear much fruit, showing yourselves to be my disciples.*

Giving

Malachi 3:10 *Bring the whole tithe into the storehouse, that there may be food in my house. Test me in this," says the LORD Almighty, "and see if I will not throw open the floodgates of heaven and pour out so much blessing that you will not have room enough for it.*

Godliness

Titus 2:11-14 *For the grace of God that brings salvation has appeared to all men. It teaches us to say*

"No" to ungodliness and worldly passions, and to live self-controlled, upright and godly lives in this present age, while we wait for the blessed hope—the glorious appearing of our great God and Savior, Jesus Christ, who gave himself for us to redeem us from all wickedness and to purify for himself a people that are his very own, eager to do what is good.

Happiness

Matthew 5:3-12 *"Blessed are the poor in spirit, for theirs is the kingdom of heaven. Blessed are those who mourn, for they will be comforted. Blessed are the meek, for they will inherit the earth. Blessed are those who hunger and thirst for righteousness, for they will be filled. Blessed are the merciful, for they will be shown mercy. Blessed are the pure in heart, for they will see God. Blessed are the peacemakers, for they will be called sons of God. Blessed are those who are persecuted because of righteousness, for theirs is the kingdom of heaven. "Blessed are you when people insult you, persecute you and falsely say all kinds of evil against you because of me. Rejoice and be glad, because great is your reward in heaven, for in the same way they persecuted the prophets who were before you.*

Healing

James 5:13-16 *[13]Is any one of you in trouble? He should pray. Is anyone happy? Let him sing songs of praise. [14]Is any one of you sick? He should call the elders of the church to pray over him and anoint him with oil in the name of the Lord.* ¹⁵*And the prayer offered in faith will make the sick person well; the Lord will raise him up. If he has sinned, he will be forgiven.* ¹⁶*Therefore confess your sins to each other and pray for each other so that you may be healed. The prayer of a righteous man is powerful and effective.*

1 Peter 2:24*"He himself bore our sins" in his body on the cross, so that we might die to sins and live for righteousness; "by his wounds you have been healed."*

Exodus 15:26 *He said, "If you listen carefully to the voice of the LORD your God and do what is right in his eyes, if you pay attention to his commands and keep all his decrees, I will not bring on you any of the diseases I brought on the Egyptians, for I am the LORD, who heals you."*

Holiness

1 Peter 1:13-16 *Therefore, prepare your minds for action; be self-controlled; set your hope fully on the grace to be given you when Jesus Christ is revealed. As obedient children, do not conform to the evil desires you had when you lived in ignorance. But just as he who called you is holy, so be holy in all you do; for it is written: "Be holy, because I am holy."*

2 Peter 1:3 *His divine power has given us everything we need for a godly life through our knowledge of him who called us by his own glory and goodness.*

Honesty

2 Corinthians 8:21 *For we are taking pains to do what is right, not only in the eyes of the Lord but also in the eyes of men.*

Honoring Your Parents And Others

Ephesians 6:1-3 *Children, obey your parents in the Lord, for this is right. "Honor your father and mother"— which is the first commandment with a promise— "that it may go well with you and that you may enjoy long life on the earth*

1 Peter 2:17 *Show proper respect to everyone: Love the brotherhood of believers, fear God, honor the king.*

Hope

1 Peter 1:13 *Therefore, prepare your minds for action; be self-controlled; set your hope fully on the grace to be given you when Jesus Christ is revealed.*

Isaiah 40:31 *But those who hope in the LORD will renew their strength. They will soar on wings like eagles; they will run and not grow weary, they will walk and not be faint.*

Jeremiah 29:11 *For I know the plans I have for you,"
declares the LORD, "plans to prosper you and not to
harm you, plans to give you hope and a future.*

Psalm 25:5 *Guide me in your truth and teach me, for
you are God my Savior, and my hope is in you all day
long.*

Humility

Luke 18:9-14 *To some who were confident of their
own righteousness and looked down on everybody else,
Jesus told this parable: "Two men went up to the temple
to pray, one a Pharisee and the other a tax collector. The
Pharisee stood up and prayed about[a] himself: 'God, I
thank you that I am not like other men—robbers,
evildoers, adulterers — or even like this tax collector. I
fast twice a week and give a tenth of all I get.' "But the
tax collector stood at a distance. He would not even look
up to heaven, but beat his breast and said, 'God, have
mercy on me, a sinner.'" I tell you that this man, rather
than the other, went home justified before God. For
everyone who exalts himself will be humbled, and he who
humbles himself will be exalted."*

Philippians 2:3-11 *Do nothing out of selfish ambition
or vain conceit, but in humility consider others better
than yourselves. Each of you should look not only to your
own interests, but also to the interests of others. Your
attitude should be the same as that of Christ Jesus: Who,
being in very nature God, did not consider equality with*

God something to be grasped, but made himself nothing, taking the very nature of a servant, being made in human likeness. And being found in appearance as a man, he humbled himself and became obedient to death — even death on a cross! Therefore God exalted him to the highest place and gave him the name that is above every name, that at the name of Jesus every knee should bow, in heaven and on earth and under the earth, and every tongue confess that Jesus Christ is Lord, to the glory of God the Father.

Joy

Luke 10:20 *However, do not rejoice that the spirits submit to you, but rejoice that your names are written in heaven.*

Philippians 4:4 *Rejoice in the Lord always. I will say it again: Rejoice!*

John 15:11 *I have told you this so that my joy may be in you and that your joy may be complete.*

Kindness

Colossians 3:12-13 *Therefore, as God's chosen people, holy and dearly loved, clothe yourselves with compassion, kindness, humility, gentleness and patience. 13Bear with each other and forgive whatever grievances you may have against one another. Forgive as the Lord forgave you.*

Labor

John 9:4 *As long as it is day, we must do the work of him who sent me. Night is coming, when no one can work.*

Love

1 John 4:8 *Whoever does not love does not know God, because God is love.*

Luke 10:27 *He answered: 'Love the Lord your God with all your heart and with all your soul and with all your strength and with all your mind'; and, 'Love your neighbor as yourself.'*

1 Corinthians 13 *If I speak in the tongues of men and of angels, but have not love, I am only a resounding gong or a clanging cymbal. If I have the gift of prophecy and can fathom all mysteries and all knowledge, and if I have a faith that can move mountains, but have not love, I am nothing. If I give all I possess to the poor and surrender my body to the flames, but have not love, I gain nothing. Love is patient, love is kind. It does not envy, it does not boast, it is not proud. It is not rude, it is not self-seeking, it is not easily angered, it keeps no record of wrongs. Love does not delight in evil but rejoices with the truth. It always protects, always trusts, always hopes, always perseveres. Love never fails. But where there are prophecies, they will cease; where there are tongues, they will be stilled; where there is knowledge, it will pass*

away. For we know in part and we prophesy in part, but when perfection comes, the imperfect disappears. When I was a child, I talked like a child, I thought like a child, I reasoned like a child. When I became a man, I put childish ways behind me. Now we see but a poor reflection as in a mirror; then we shall see face to face. Now I know in part; then I shall know fully, even as I am fully known. And now these three remain: faith, hope and love. But the greatest of these is love.

Obedience

John 14:15-24 *"If you love me, you will obey what I command. And I will ask the Father, and he will give you another Counselor to be with you forever— the Spirit of truth. The world cannot accept him, because it neither sees him nor knows him. But you know him, for he lives with you and will be in you. I will not leave you as orphans; I will come to you. Before long, the world will not see me anymore, but you will see me. Because I live, you also will live. On that day you will realize that I am in my Father, and you are in me, and I am in you. Whoever has my commands and obeys them, he is the one who loves me. He who loves me will be loved by my Father, and I too will love him and show myself to him."* *Then Judas (not Judas Iscariot) said, "But, Lord, why do you intend to show yourself to us and not to the world?"* *Jesus replied, "If anyone loves me, he will obey my teaching. My Father will love him, and we will come to him and make our home with him. He who does not love me will not obey my teaching. These words you hear are not my own; they belong to the Father who sent me.*

Acts 5:29 *Peter and the other apostles replied: "We must obey God rather than men!*

Overcoming

John 16:33 *"I have told you these things, so that in me you may have peace. In this world you will have trouble. But take heart! I have overcome the world."*

Patience

Hebrews 10:36 *You need to persevere so that when you have done the will of God, you will receive what he has promised.*

Peacefulness

John 14:27 *Peace I leave with you; my peace I give you. I do not give to you as the world gives. Do not let your hearts be troubled and do not be afraid.*

Romans 12:18 *If it is possible, as far as it depends on you, live at peace with everyone.*

Perseverance

Mark 13:5-13 *Jesus said to them: "Watch out that no one deceives you. Many will come in my name, claiming, 'I am he,' and will deceive many. When you hear of wars and rumors of wars, do not be alarmed. Such things must happen, but the end is still to come. Nation will rise against nation and kingdom against kingdom. There will be earthquakes in various places, and famines. These are the beginning of birth pains. "You must be on your guard. You will be handed over to the local councils and flogged in the synagogues. On account of me you will stand before governors and kings as witnesses to them. And the gospel must first be preached to all nations. Whenever you are arrested and brought to trial, do not worry beforehand about what to say. Just say whatever is given you at the time, for it is not you speaking, but the Holy Spirit." Brother will betray brother to death and a father his child. Children will rebel against their parents and have them put to death. All men will hate you because of me, but he who stands firm to the end will be saved.*

Prayer

Luke 11:1-13 *One day Jesus was praying in a certain place. When he finished, one of his disciples said to him, "Lord, teach us to pray, just as John taught his disciples." He said to them, "When you pray, say:" 'Father, hallowed be your name, your kingdom come. Give us each day our daily bread. Forgive us our sins, for we also forgive everyone who sins against us. And lead us not into temptation.' "Then he said to them, "Suppose one of you has a friend, and he goes to him at midnight and says, 'Friend, lend me three loaves of bread, because a friend of mine on a journey has come to me, and I have nothing to set before him.'" Then the one inside answers, 'Don't bother me. The door is already locked, and my children are with me in bed. I can't get up and give you anything.' I tell you, though he will not get up and give him the bread because he is his friend, yet because of the man's boldness he will get up and give him as much as he needs. "So I say to you: Ask and it will be given to you; seek and you will find; knock and the door will be opened to you. For everyone who asks receives; he who seeks finds; and to him who knocks, the door will be opened. "Which of you fathers, if your son asks for a fish, will give him a snake instead? Or if he asks for an egg, will give him a scorpion? If you then, though you are evil, know how to give good gifts to your children, how much more will your Father in heaven give the Holy Spirit to those who ask him!"*

Ephesians 6:18 *And pray in the Spirit on all occasions with all kinds of prayers and requests. With this in mind, be alert and always keep on praying for all the saints.*

Pure thinking

Philippians 4:8 *Finally, brothers, whatever is true, whatever is noble, whatever is right, whatever is pure, whatever is lovely, whatever is admirable—if anything is excellent or praiseworthy—think about such things.*

Purity

Matthew 5:27-32 *You have heard that it was said, 'Do not commit adultery.' But I tell you that anyone who looks at a woman lustfully has already committed adultery with her in his heart. If your right eye causes you to sin, gouge it out and throw it away. It is better for you to lose one part of your body than for your whole body to be thrown into hell. And if your right hand causes you to sin, cut it off and throw it away. It is better for you to lose one part of your body than for your whole body to go into hell. "It has been said, 'Anyone who divorces his wife must give her a certificate of divorce.' But I tell you that anyone who divorces his wife, except for marital unfaithfulness, causes her to become an adulteress, and anyone who marries the divorced woman commits adultery*

2 Timothy 2:22 *Flee the evil desires of youth, and pursue righteousness, faith, love and peace, along with those who call on the Lord out of a pure heart.*

Reading the Bible

John 5:39 *You diligently study[a] the Scriptures because you think that by them you possess eternal life. These are the Scriptures that testify about me.*

Psalm 1:2 *But his delight is in the law of the LORD, and on his law he meditates day and night.*

Psalm 119:97 *Oh, how I love your law! I meditate on it all day long.*

John 15:7 *If you remain in me and my words remain in you, ask whatever you wish, and it will be given you.*

Joshua 1:8 *Do not let this Book of the Law depart from your mouth; meditate on it day and night, so that you may be careful to do everything written in it. Then you will be prosperous and successful.*

Romans 12:2 (KJV) *And be not conformed to this world: but be ye transformed by the renewing of your mind, that ye may prove what is that good, and acceptable, and perfect, will of God.*

Resolution

Ephesians 6:10-18 *Finally, be strong in the Lord and in his mighty power. Put on the full armor of God so that you can take your stand against the devil's schemes. For our struggle is not against flesh and blood, but against the rulers, against the authorities, against the powers of this dark world and against the spiritual forces of evil in the heavenly realms. Therefore put on the full armor of God, so that when the day of evil comes, you may be able to stand your ground, and after you have done everything, to stand. Stand firm then, with the belt of truth buckled around your waist, with the breastplate of righteousness in place, and with your feet fitted with the readiness that comes from the gospel of peace. In addition to all this, take up the shield of faith, with which you can extinguish all the flaming arrows of the evil one. Take the helmet of salvation and the sword of the Spirit, which is the word of God. And pray in the Spirit on all occasions with all kinds of prayers and requests. With this in mind, be alert and always keep on praying for all the saints.*

Righteousness

Matthew 5:6 *Blessed are those who hunger and thirst for righteousness, for they will be filled.*

Matthew 6:33 *But seek first his kingdom and his righteousness, and all these things will be given to you as well.*

Sincerity

Philippians 1:9-10 *And this is my prayer: that your love may abound more and more in knowledge and depth of insight, so that you may be able to discern what is best and may be pure and blameless until the day of Christ,*

Steadfastness

1 Corinthians 15:58 *Therefore, my dear brothers, stand firm. Let nothing move you. Always give yourselves fully to the work of the Lord, because you know that your labor in the Lord is not in vain.*

Job 21:22 *Can anyone teach knowledge to God, since he judges even the highest?*

Galatians 6:7 *Do not be deceived: God cannot be mocked. People reap what they sow.*

Stewardship

1 Corinthians 4:2 *Now it is required that those who have been given a trust must prove faithful.*

2 Corinthians 9:6-7 *Remember this: Whoever sows sparingly will also reap sparingly, and whoever sows generously will also reap generously. Each man should give what he has decided in his heart to give, not reluctantly or under compulsion, for God loves a cheerful giver.*

Temperance

1 Thessalonians 5:6-8 *So then, let us not be like others, who are asleep, but let us be alert and self-controlled. For those who sleep, sleep at night, and those who get drunk, get drunk at night. But since we belong to the day, let us be self-controlled, putting on faith and love as a breastplate, and the hope of salvation as a helmet.*

Trust

Psalm 37:3-5 *Trust in the LORD and do good; dwell in the land and enjoy safe pasture. Delight yourself in the LORD and he will give you the desires of your heart. Commit your way to the LORD; trust in him and he will do this*

Proverbs 3:5-6 *Trust in the LORD with all your heart and lean not on your own understanding; in all your ways acknowledge him, and he will make your paths straight.*

Truth

John 14:6 *Jesus answered, "I am the way and the truth and the life. No one comes to the Father except through me.*

John 17:17 *Sanctify them by the truth; your word is truth.*

Ephesians 4:14-15 *Then we will no longer be infants, tossed back and forth by the waves, and blown here and there by every wind of teaching and by the cunning and craftiness of men in their deceitful scheming. Instead, speaking the truth in love, we will in all things grow up into him who is the Head, that is, Christ.*

Philippians 4:8 *Finally, brothers, whatever is true, whatever is noble, whatever is right, whatever is pure, whatever is lovely, whatever is admirable—if anything is excellent or praiseworthy—think about such things.*

Victory

1 Corinthians 15:57 *But thanks be to God! He gives us the victory through our Lord Jesus Christ.*

1 John 5:4 *for everyone born of God overcomes the world. This is the victory that has overcome the world, even our faith.*

Watchfulness

Mark 13:34-37 *It's like a man going away: He leaves his house and puts his servants in charge, each with his assigned task, and tells the one at the door to keep watch." Therefore keep watch because you do not know when the owner of the house will come back—whether in the evening, or at midnight, or when the rooster crows, or at dawn. If he comes suddenly, do not let him find you sleeping. What I say to you, I say to everyone: 'Watch!'*

Worship

John 4:23-24 *Yet a time is coming and has now come when the true worshipers will worship the Father in spirit and truth, for they are the kind of worshipers the Father seeks. 24 God is spirit, and his worshipers must worship in spirit and in truth."*

Zeal

Romans 12:11 *Never be lacking in zeal, but keep your spiritual fervor, serving the Lord.*

141

Chapter 9

Are you going to Heaven?

John 14:6 *Jesus answered, "I am the way and the truth and the life. No one comes to the Father except through me.*

We see in the above scripture that Jesus the son of God is the only way to get to the Father which is in Heaven. He is the bridge that connects us to the Father, we must pass through.

The living words of God in the Bible also declare in the book of John 3:16 that we must believe in Jesus, so we will not perish and have everlasting life.

John 3:16 (KJV) *[16]For God so loved the world, that he gave his only begotten Son, that whosoever believeth in him should not perish, but have everlasting life.*

The living words of God in the Bible also declare in the book of Romans 10:9 (KJV) *That if thou shalt confess with thy mouth the Lord Jesus, and shalt believe in thine heart that God hath raised him from the dead, thou shalt be saved.* And also in the book of 1 John 1:9, the Bible declares that, *If we confess our sins, he is faithful and just and will forgive us our sins and purify us from all unrighteousness.*

So if you are not sure you're saved and going to heaven and want to be sure without a doubt, please pray this simple prayer with me;

Dear Jesus, I ask you to come and dwell into my heart as my Lord and savior. Forgive and cleanse me from all of my sins. I confess with my mouth and believe in my heart, that you died for all my sins and that you were raised from the dead on the third day by God the Father. In Jesus mighty name, Amen

If you said this simple prayer, welcome to the body of Christ. Praise the Lord! You are now saved and going to heaven. The next step to do is get a good study Bible and find a good Bible based church and start meditating daily on God's living words.

Also the living words of God in the Bible, in the book of Acts 2:38 declares that, *Peter replied, "Repent and be baptized, every one of you, in the name of Jesus Christ for the forgiveness of your sins. And you will receive the gift of the Holy Spirit.*

If this book has help you to know and understand God and the living words of God, so that you can begin living a life of true peace, true love, true joy and true happiness here on earth, until your in Heaven, please recommend it to other people. May the spirit of the Lord be with you and your family always. God bless you!

Keep moving forwards towards your goal in life with a deep loving passion and a relentless conviction of knowing you will get there eventually.

~Michael Anthony Gagliardi~

God and His Living Words are the same Yesterday, Today and Forever, so Stand Still and See the Salvation of the Lord. The Victory Is Yours!

~Michael Anthony Gagliardi~

LaVergne, TN USA
25 February 2011

217813LV00001B/40/P